God's Infinite Lov... ...has been said of it. This work can be read with profit by sinner and saint, and by those of the intervening stages." It describes the charm, happiness and delight of divine love, not forgetting to point out where the lion seeks his prey, and the wolf has its lair. It does not, it is true, follow the stereotype method of books on this subject, but the author claims that while guiding his readers, by a sure and safe path, he invites them to admire the scenery, perceive the odour of the flowers, and partake of the delicious fruit.

But as love, to be genuine, must be mutual, many of the pages here are devoted to training the soul in the ways of divine love. The goal is union with God, acquired by that love which unites the human will with the divine. Nothing here is too sublime for the ordinary Christian to desire; nothing too insignificant for the more advanced to neglect.

To-day, when there is such an incessant war waged upon God, it is imperative that all of goodwill be armed with weapons of defence, forged in the furnace of truth. In these pages such will be found in abundance, and in the day of need will prove of the greatest advantage.

This book, it is hoped, will cast a ray of sunshine on dark and evil days, and throw a mantle of joy over the humdrum events of daily life.

GOD'S INFINITE LOVE AND OURS

God's Infinite Love and Ours

By

ROBERT MAGEEAN, C.SS.R.

"God is Charity, and he that Abideth in Charity,
Abideth in God and God in him."

(1 John iv, 16).

DUBLIN
CLONMORE AND REYNOLDS LTD.
LONDON
BURNS OATES AND WASHBOURNE LIMITED

First Published 1957

De Licentia Superiorum Ordinis : MICHAEL CURRAN, C.SS.R., Supr. Prov.
Nihil Obstat : CORNELIUS F.LEE, Censor Deputatus.
Imprimatur : ✠ JOANNES CAROLUS, ARCHIEPISCOPUS DUBLINEN.
Hibernae Primas, 15-3-1957.

Made and Printed in the Republic of Ireland
FOR
CLONMORE AND REYNOLDS LIMITED
BY HELY'S LIMITED, DUBLIN

CONTENTS

CONTENTS

INTRODUCTION

DIVINE LOVE is an eternal theme; it commenced in the depths of eternity before the creation of the world, when the Father, Son and Holy Ghost, by a spiritual embrace, unite in infinite love. It was heard in heaven, when St. Michael exclaiming: "Who is like unto God?" drew the elect angels in his train, and cast out Lucifer for ever. Moses recommended this love to the Jewish people, promising a rich reward to those who cultivated it; David poured forth his psalms in admiration of it, and the author of the Canticle of Canticles praised it wholeheartedly. But it was reserved for the New Law, in which love has supplanted fear, to pay a fitting tribute to charity. St. Paul, in verses of surpassing beauty, has described it as the excellent way leading to heaven. (1 Cor. xiii, 1, 3-8).

St. Augustine's Confessions are a treatise, and a very excellent one, on the love of God. St. Bernard in his discourses on the Canticles, has, with lips touched with celestial fire, described the nature and effects of charity, and this if we except the inspired writings, is probably the most perfect treatise we have on divine love. Thomas Aquinas, shortly before his death, exhausted his learning and affections in explaining the same inspired work, while Gerson, one time Chancellor of the University of Paris, received the unstinted praise of Sixtus of Siena for his description of the qualities of divine love, as found in these Canticles. St. Bonaventure, in his "Goad of Divine Love," has shown us how, by reflecting on the Passion of Christ, we may inflame our hearts with the fervour of its ardent flames.

It is the hope of the present writer to make, by this book, the love of God appreciated and cultivated by all. In labouring to do so, I believe I am following the Divine Exemplar, who said: "I have come to cast fire on the earth, and what will I but that it be kindled?" (Luke xii, 49). This is a book, written in a popular style, explaining a system which all can reduce to practice. It was to such a love of God, Christ gave everyone an invitation, when He said: "Be you therefore perfect as also your heavenly Father is perfect." (Matt. v, 48).

The genuine love of God is the best means of counteracting the false systems of religion afloat in the world to-day. These false doctrines are so destructive that they would, if possible, extinguish the last spark of Christianity.

CHAPTER I

What is Love?

SOME MAY consider it strange that a book treating of the love of God should commence with a discussion on love in general. Yet there are excellent reasons for so doing, and among them are two which should make a special appeal. In the first place, natural and supernatural love are exercised by the same faculty, the will, and as grace does not destroy but perfects nature, it follows that if we grasp how the will acts in natural, we shall understand how it acts in supernatural love. In the next place, by realising what supernatural love is not, we shall the more easily learn what it is. Now, natural, as also that which is passionate, are not supernatural. Consequently by eliminating these two we shall see exactly where supernatural love begins.

Love, in its earliest stages, is the sweetness experienced by the will in embracing the object it desires. This causes satisfaction. As a bee commences life, is developed and nurtured in honey, so love springs from, is developed and nurtured by complacency.

Soon a habit is formed. This after some time makes it pleasant and easy to perform acts that manifest love. These consist naturally in the bestowal of gifts,[1] that make the lover and the loved one happy. Yet such gifts must be mutual; for if the recipient fail to express gratitude by making a suitable return, the other will consider him selfish, cease to cherish affection, and will allow love to disappear altogether.

[1] St. Alphonsus: "Praxis Amandi Jesum Christum" 23, says: "As Almighty God knew that man is won by kindness, he determined to lavish His gifts on him, and so take captive the affections of his heart."

Love is universal; but it exists only between persons, between man and man, between woman and woman, as well as man and woman. An example of the first, which I will now explain at some length, as it is a model for all to imitate, is that between Jonathan and David, of the second is the love of Ruth for Naomi, as related in the Bible, and of the third of Abraham for his wife Sarah.

THE FRIENDSHIP OF DAVID AND JONATHAN

We read in the First Book of Kings that between David and Jonathan a cherished friendship arose. Their love was strong, upright, pure, faithful till death, and conferred inestimable blessings on both. Saul, learning that David had been appointed to supplant him as king of Israel, conceived a bitter hatred for him, and resolved to put him to death. This was not hidden from David; for some time previously when the younger man was singing in presence of Saul, the latter, with the intention of impaling him against the wall, hurled a spear at David. At their next meeting he told Jonathan how things stood. Jonathan refused to believe it, but resolved to find out the truth. Soon he discovered that David's suspicions were right, and persuaded his friend to retire into solitude. In this way Jonathan saved his life. At the same time David promised to protect Jonathan's children. Such good services cemented their friendship, and it remained steadfast both in life and death.

When Jonathan was killed in battle David sang over him:

"How are the valiant fallen in battle? Jonathan slain in the high places?

"I grieve for thee my brother Jonathan, exceeding beautiful and amiable to me above the love of woman. As a mother loveth her only son, so do I love thee." (11 Kings 1, 25, 26).

THE FOUNDATION OF LOVE

The foundation on which love is based is the partaking of the same life and society. The gifts bestowed are an invitation to enjoy such life and society. They assume then, in the eyes of the one who receives them, a value and importance they would not otherwise possess.

As regards love in general, we can verify this by daily experience. Each one of us has friends whom we love in a special way. When we examine our feelings towards them we shall find that we are of interest to them and they to us, as long as we are careful to attend to such acts as manifest affection. No eye is more keen, no heart more jealous, than those of the lover. The slightest neglect is noticed, the least impropriety dwelt on and magnified, and yet did it happen with others, it would be passed by as insignificant. This neglect will render visits rarer; the loved one will no longer be considered part of oneself; and separation will follow.

But in the case of divine love, though natural gifts may prepare the way, they are certainly no part of it; for it is the immediate result of sanctifying grace. Such grace so unites us to God as to enable us, while living on this earth, to participate in divine life and happiness. Now, the life of God is a life of knowledge, of love, and the eternal blessedness that accompany these. The Eternal Father, by knowing perfectly His divine essence, begets the Son, and from the natural love of Father and Son, which is infinite, proceeds the Holy Ghost. But how can we, so strongly inclined as we are to sin, participate in so glorious, so eternal a life? Not by our own merits but by the merits of Jesus Christ. For Jesus is God. And this has rendered it easy for all to be united to God, and participate in His divine life; for in some mysterious way, as St. Athanasius asserts, the Incarnation has sanctified all flesh. St. Peter in his Second Epistle (1, 2-4) has expressed this beautifully: "Grace to you and peace be accomplished in the knowledge of God, and of

Christ Jesus our Lord: As all things of His divine power, which pertain to life and godliness are given us, through the knowledge of Him who hath called us by His own glory and virtue, by whom He hath given us most great and precious promises that *by these you may be made partakers of the divine nature.*"

This union, acquired by sanctifying grace, is a supernatural habit, abiding permanently in the soul, enabling it to perform acts that merit eternal life. It differs from actual grace which is but a passing aid that enlightens the mind and arouses the will to produce such acts. Sanctifying grace has been justly called "the seed of God"; for in it, as the future oak in the acorn, is contained the heavenly reward, the right to the Beatific Vision. This grace, on entering the soul, brings an array of other gifts; a superior knowledge and deeper love of God and one's neighbour, a Christian life of holiness, the incorporation in Christ, and the indwelling of the Holy Ghost. By these gifts we are renewed, and made quite different from what we were. "Put on the new man," says St. Paul, "who according to God is created in justice and holiness of truth." (Eph. iv, 24).

Since Our Lord is the author of sanctifying grace, no one knows its nature and necessity better than He. We are not surprised to find Him make use of a parable to explain its importance. (Luke xiii).

The following example will illustrate what has been said:

Often have we seen a lake lit up, and shining beneath the rays of a summer's sun. The sun clothes it, so to say, with a garment of light; for all the waters gleam with a sweet radiance, nay, in the heart of the lake is reflected an image of the sun. But perhaps there is nothing more delightful and productive than the heat it produces. To this heat we may liken divine charity. It causes the vegetation of spiritual life, the flowers of good desires, the fruit of solid virtue, to spring up in the soul.

Its chief result is to unite the will of man, with the will of God; it aims at unifying the two wills. What is the result? The soul takes a delight in the union, which will make it pleasant for the human will to submit, and carry out the behests and the desires of God. "You have not received the spirit of bondage again in fear; but you have received the spirit of adoption whereby we cry: Abba (Father)." (Rom. viii, 15).

THE INTELLECT AND THE WILL

Charity resides in the will. It is therefore very essential to distinguish between these two faculties of the soul—intellect and will.

All persons we find on this planet have souls, a truth that can be made clear by reason itself. That they have rational souls is deduced from the fact that they can conceive and express general or universal ideas. We know, for instance, that the saying:

"To err is human, to forgive divine—"
is always and everywhere true; for so weak is man, so merciful is the Almighty, that there never was and never will be a time, but human nature on this earth could[1] err, and that God could forgive the erring. And all languages are full of such proverbs, proceeding from the intelligence of man; for it is men and women not animals that give such proverbs.

These souls are simple, spiritual substances. They can reason and acquire a knowledge of a world beyond the present, can grasp that this is a place of trial, because here the good frequently suffer and the wicked prosper, and that it will require the scales of justice to make right such incongruities. Therefore such people have intellects, and wherever there is an intellect there is a will; for we know that when the intellect understands that a

[1] The word "could" is here used advisedly; for though Christ had no sin, yet Suarez says Christ was free, but any possibility of sin in Him could never be reduced to act.

thing is good, another faculty—the will—immediately rushes forth to embrace it.

Yet the will is free. If not, why should parents be at such trouble to have their children properly educated, so as to think aright, and so conduct themselves as to be a credit to parents and country. Corresponding to the mind or intellect in the soul, there is a brain in the body, and some have foolishly declared that it thinks. But the brain being a material substance cannot excogitate spiritual ideas; the effect cannot be greater than the cause; spiritual ideas must spring from the faculty of a spiritual substance.

What causes us all to realise the existence of the will is that at times we are pained to see a self-willed child, on being told to obey, stamp the floor with its foot, crying "I will not."

But the will need not, nay, should not be obstinate; it should be docile, and when it is, it can achieve a world of good. But to be so it must be trained to acts of virtue, and especially to acts of divine charity. This training will direct its waywardness into the right channels and will teach it to use its freedom. But we must be prepared for surprises and disappointments. Simply because the will is free, it can and may under a strong temptation reject the better and choose the worse motive. Not only does the word of God assure us of this in many places (Deut. xxvi, 17, 18; John vi, 68) but our common sense does the same, for we know we can, if we will, avoid evil and do good.

But if we would understand thoroughly the nature of divine love, we must consider it in its various kinds, where we can examine it from its inception to its perfection.

THE DIFFERENT KINDS OF LOVE

Love in its simplest form is that of a child for its mother. She, by instinct, has a tender affection for the child of her womb, and expresses it in smiles, embraces and acts of kindness.

The child, though not yet gifted with reason, notices such endearments, is pleased with them, and returns the affection. Such favours, coming constantly from the mother, make the child realise who its best friend is. In course of time its attachment becomes a settled habit, and this grows with the dawn of reason. At length it loves its mother, because she is so good, affectionate and gentle. At this stage the child begins to imitate her, who is its ideal, whose words and acts it admires.

This love on the part of a child, who has attained the use of reason, is a natural virtue. It is good; but as it does not spring from faith, cannot, till the supernatural motive is introduced, gain an eternal reward. This supernatural motive will bring the virtue infused by Baptism into operation, and cause its acts to merit heaven.

But besides natural love, there is also love which is a passion. It is an attraction between the sexes, placed there by nature for the mutual support of those who have it, and for the propagation of the human race. This love also, unless supernaturalised by a supernatural motive, remains a purely natural affection. But the children, the mother and father, who take the Holy Family, Jesus, Mary and Joseph, as their models, elevate their love to the supernatural order.

In addition to these there is the supernatural love of God, by which we love Him, because of the gifts He bestows. Such imperfect love is termed the love of chaste desire. It is good and merits a reward, yet is more correctly termed hope than charity. But such love does not, as some have foolishly imagined, weaken charity. In fact, it strengthens it, even though we have already far advanced in the virtue of divine love; for it assists the weakness of human nature, to begin with the lower forms, and advance to the higher.

An example will illustrate the nature and advantage of this kind of love.

We read in the life of St. Augustine that, when he was a sinner, addicted to a disreputable vice, he entertained a tender affection for his mother, St. Monica. She returned it. In her case, it was supernatural; for she wept, prayed, did penance for the conversion of her son. It was a victory won ultimately at the cost of her wholehearted self-sacrifice. She conquered. She succeeded in making him the child and Doctor of grace; through her he received many favours from God, and profitted by them and ultimately explained the Catholic doctrine on grace with a lucidity and consideration, that will to the end of time enlighten orthodox teachers, and conquer heresy. After abandoning the occasion of sin, that had for so long held him captive, he began to love God with that heroic and seraphic love, that has made him one of the greatest Saints and Doctors of the Church.

BENEVOLENCE

Benevolence! What a big word, and yet when explained how simple! It means good-will or wishing well to another. When we have grasped, even in a vague way, the infinite goodness of God, from which His benefits unceasingly flow, we are moved to wish well to so generous a Benefactor. We sing His praises in hymns of joy, wish Him all the glory possible, rejoice that He is infinitely happy, and that He is loved in heaven as He deserves. In this way the human heart is brought to overflow with delight, and the soul, at the thought of the infinite goodness of God, becomes enraptured with joy. It then makes use of some of the beautiful hymns of praise to be found in our Catholic Manuals. The Gloria, which is said at Mass, and a translation of which is found in many prayer-books, is one of the most perfect hymns we can recite in praise of God. We find it quoted by St. Athanasius of the fourth century as a prayer suitable for virgins. The divine praises, recited after Benediction of the Blessed Sacrament, is also a prayer of marvellous beauty and unction.

When we have the love of benevolence towards God in our hearts, we have charity; for with it we have friendship. St. Thomas teaches that charity is reached when we have mutual benevolence with an interchange of goods. When we love God, we know for certain He loves us; "I love them that love Me." (Prov. viii, 17). And the blessings He bestows on those who wish Him well are innumerable; for He says: "With Me are riches and glory . . . that I may enrich them that love Me." (Prov. viii, 12). And the heart that truly loves God takes care to make some return of gratitude for favours received. "They that fear the Lord will seek after things that are well pleasing to Him, and they that love Him shall be filled with His law." (Eccl. ii, 19). What better return could we make God for all He has done for us than to keep His Commandments, to be exact in fulfilling His will? But we shall have occasion to treat of this later, and shall say no more about it here.

LOVE OF FRIENDSHIP

Friendship towards God and man, must, for social beings like us, hold an important place. Much of our happiness and misery come from associating with others, yet much of this misery can be eliminated by cultivating true friendship. He who has found a genuine friend has found a treasure, and should be prepared to sacrifice much to preserve his (*amicitia*) affection.

Friendship for God is the soul of charity; supernatural friendship for our neighbour is, when perfect, the direct result of divine charity, but when imperfect is a step leading to the pure love of God. By it we love God above all things for His own sake, and our neighbour as ourselves for God's sake. The least particle of this divine friendship takes away all sin, at least all serious sin. Were the greatest sinner on the point of death to elicit such an act, he would escape the flames of hell. It is a disputed point as to whether the love of God, from the view-point of gratitude, or one divine attribute, wisdom, truth, purity, is perfect contrition. It is probable that it is, though the teaching of St. Thomas and St. Alphonsus demands that the motive include in a general way the complexus of all the divine perfections. However, it could be used as a first step, from which we could easily proceed to the more perfect motive. Let us not forget that perfect charity, friendship for God, depends on the perfection of the motive.

ST. AELRED ON FRIENDSHIP

We find in St. Aelred of Rievoulx an example of one who had a genius for friendship, not only for the love of God, but also for that of his fellow-men. He wrote a work entitled: "Christian Friendship," which portrays faithfully the warm affection burning in his own soul. From it we make the following quotation, which emphasises the necessity of spiritual friendship.

"True friendship, which is definitely genuine, is spiritual. It has not as its motive any self-seeking. It is cultivated for its own intrinsic worth, and because it fundamentally satisfies the human heart. The advantages and rewards to be gained from spiritual friendship consist in cultivating it, and nothing else. This is why Our Lord said in the Gospel: 'I have chosen you to go and bring forth fruit,' that is to love one another. True friendship grows ever deeper and deeper, and its fruit consists in the enjoyment of its full perfection, so that the precept of loving one another is strictly observed. So spiritual friendship takes its rise in good people, from similarity of outlook, ideals and tastes. In other words it is perfect agreement on things sacred and profane, accompanied by benevolence and love."[1]

THE TEACHING OF ST. THOMAS

Although what has already been outlined in the foregoing

[1] Christian Friendship, p. 44.

pages is in harmony with the teaching of the Angelic Doctor, it may be acceptable to many to have the doctrine of St. Thomas exactly as he explains it, on this subject.[1]

St. Thomas explains clearly that love is an attraction to some good thing. Attractions, however, are well nigh universal, being found in animal as well as in intellectual nature. But the love infused by God into the will, and founded on the communication of supernatural goods, which is nothing else than a participation in the happiness of God Himself, constitutes the virtue of charity. This virtue needs the light derived from faith, and the trust inspired by hope.

As regards the virtue itself, St. Thomas states it is a super-natural quality residing in the will. As supernatural it springs from grace, and from the revealed motive of God's goodness in Himself; it is an accident which modifies the substance in which it inheres. This quality is increased by the more abundant graces bestowed, which enable it to embrace a greater number of deserving objects, and to do so with greater intensity.

It is founded on the communication of divine gifts. These lead the soul to greater intimacy with God. Since God is an infinitely pure spirit the only union that can obtain between Him and the soul is an intellectual one. The will, a blind faculty, is the rational appetite, depending for guidance on the light of the intellect. In this way God and the human will become one: "He who is joined to the Lord is one spirit." (1 Cor. vi, 17). And now God comes and dwells in the soul, as in His own temple: "Know you not that you are the temple of God, and that the spirit of God dwelleth in you." (1 Cor. iii, 16). The soul now becomes enraptured with the presence of God and is sometimes so entranced, and beside herself with love, that ecstasy is the result. This love at the same time inflames the

---

[1] His teaching is found in the following works: Sum. Theol., i, ii, q. 26-8: iii Sent. d. 27. 1. q. i; Contra Gent. iv, 19; Quodlib. i, a. 8.

soul with a burning zeal, which labours wholeheartedly to promote the divine glory, and save souls. And because it cannot in this life be perfectly united with the God it loves, it suffers, by reason of the separation, a longing, a weariness, a pain, which is correctly termed a wound. Yet there results from the wound a delicious sense of peace and joy.

But what is the nature of the happiness God communicates to us? It is His life, perfection, and joy. Souls, far advanced in the ways of divine love, experience at times an intense delight which urges them to elicit fervent and perfect acts of love.

St. Thomas proves that if we are to have charity we must love God above all things, and our neighbours as ourselves for His sake, and shows how this is to be done, explaining at the same time the command of Jesus Christ to love God with our whole heart, our whole soul, all our strength and all our mind. We can, and should, endeavour to advance in this love all the days of our lives.

He distinguishes between the love of chaste desire, benevolence and friendship (*amicitia*).

From all this, it is clear God should come first in our lives. Nothing is to be preferred to Him. And as the expression of our love lies in the fulfilment of His will, we should endeavour to realise this as perfectly as circumstances permit.

But this does not forbid us to desire, to labour, to pray for such corporal goods as are necessary for ourselves or others. Such goods, however, as are not helpful either to the natural or supernatural life we should not desire.

Those who have the virtue of charity, and frequently practise it, will experience in their own hearts, and spread in the hearts of others, peace, joy, mercy and kindness, which will lead them to bestow on others such corporal and spiritual alms, as the needs of the neighbour demand.

They will also avoid the vices opposed to charity, which are hatred and envy of the neighbour, discord and strife among brethren, and schisms that wound the peace and unity of a community. They will seek to avoid unjust and unnecessary wars, and that spirit of strife, which is fostered by the devil; they will shun such scandals as lead the good, the simple, and all who can be drawn, from the paths of virtue.

BRIEF SYNOPSIS OF THIS WORK

We shall now, for the convenience of the reader, explain briefly the plan followed in this book, indicating how each chapter follows logically from the preceding.

In the present chapter we have explained what divine love is. For most people this would result merely in a mental exercise were it not supplemented by chapter two, in which the individual advances in divine love. This is nothing more than to reduce what has been said to practice. All our acts can, as Suarez asserts, become acts of love, if we do them from the motive of divine love. It will therefore embrace the acts of other virtues as well, for in practice charity will be weak, anaemic, unless buttressed by self-sacrifice, love of the cross, humility and conformity with God's will.

Some of the strongest motives, leading us to love God, are next developed: (1) God's goodness and mercy to us. (2) His goodness in itself. (Ch. iii). His goodness as manifested on the cross. (Ch. iv.). One of the most impelling considerations urging us to acquire as perfect a love of God as possible, is the fact that in it consists sanctity. This will lead us to strive wholeheartedly to gain the heights. (Ch. v.).

But we cannot acquire love unless we use the means. These are prayer, vocal and mental (Ch. vi), and the guardian of the spirit of prayer, which is essential if we are to advance in divine love, recollection (Ch. vii).

Work, prayer (vocal and mental) and contemplation constitute life. All these are, or at least can be made, acts of divine love. Work is sanctified by prayer and love, ordinary prayer is purified, and enriched as precious gold by divine love, and contemplation is divine love. While all are called to active, probably not all are called to *passive* contemplation (Ch. viii).

Life, whether we have it in work, ordinary prayer, or contemplation, has many consolations, which are to be used as explained in Ch. ix, but also much aridity, and patience is its remedy (Ch. x).

But we must advance in life, in sanctity, in love by greater advancements in virtue (Ch. xi) and in this way we reach the heights of perfect love of God, by perfect conformity with the divine will.

CHAPTER II

Progress in Divine Love

WE HAVE dealt with love in the abstract; we deal here with love in the concrete, with the lovers themselves. With them we plunge into a world that seethes and foams around us, having in our ears the execrations of the atheist, having before our eyes the successes and failures of life. And these circumstances unquestionably influence the development of our love for God. Blasphemy calls for reparation, immorality for purity of morals, pride for humility, self-indulgence for self-sacrifice, ill-humour for patience. The virtue of charity cannot stand alone; it must be buttressed by a variety of other virtues, otherwise it will be weak, and at the mercy of its enemies. The true lover of God is to be formed of different metal. He is to be strong, persevering, and, if God gives His grace, even heroic. But thoughts alone will not achieve this. St. John says: "Let us not love in word, nor in tongue, but in deed and in truth." (1 John iii, 18). Practice alone makes perfect.

Into this chapter then matters will be introduced which might appear to be out of place, as they would seem to come directly under other virtues, but when we remember they are necessary to uphold charity, necessary, in a very special way, for those cultivating charity, we shall be forced to admit they could not be omitted.

DEGREES OF THE LOVE OF GOD

St. Thomas teaches[1] there are three distinct degrees of charity found in those who cultivate the virtue; its beginning, its progress and perfection.

[1] ii, ii Q. 24. A.9.

In the first we shall be much concerned about avoiding sin, restraining the passions, and keeping worldly desires under control. If we fail to co-operate with grace, we do not control our appetites, mortify our senses, nor lessen our faults. On the other hand if we do correspond, we dig deeply to lay the foundations, remove a great quantity of rubble, and ultimately raise an edifice that awakens admiration. I remember once discussing this point with an old priest who had grown grey in the vineyard of the Lord. His words were wise: "If you wish to love God, and build well the castle of holiness, for love of God is holiness, you must mortify the passions thoroughly, keep senses under control, restrain a wandering imagination, and never count as lost the time spent on the work of purgation."

Here a person should learn to distinguish between deliberate and indeliberate venial sins. Deliberate are such as we advert to, know are wrong, and yet wilfully commit. All can by a little care avoid these. Indeliberate, however, such as to give way to a sudden outburst of anger, or to fail to practise a virtue when the occasion calls for it—these we can lessen, but cannot wholly eradicate. This, being one of our great crosses, makes life a true warfare. To neglect such things would primarily wound the virtue directly concerned, but it would indirectly attack charity, for if we weaken the supports of charity, we weaken charity itself. To conquer in this we need courage and self-sacrifice. But, with resolution, there is little we cannot achieve; in course of time habit renders acts of self-denial easy. At this stage a quarter of an hour's meditation, joined to examination of conscience, will work wonders. I would be far from advocating any intricate system of meditation here; the simpler, the better. It will suffice to read a spiritual book, reflect on a particular point that has struck us, and make short acts of love to God. We need not be anxious to make many different kinds of acts, for acts of divine love are the sweetest and most meritorious.

This is really to the point, for the Wise Man says: "Wisdom or charity will not enter into a malicious soul nor dwell in a body subject to sins." (Wisd. i, 4).

What has been stated should not discourage us. The way of divine love is a bright, a cheerful, a happy road to heaven. There may be clouds, but just as in nature, we shall scarcely ever find two dark days together. In fact, God to encourage souls is accustomed at this stage to deluge the generous with a flood of spiritual delights. This fills the heart with a very pleasant sensation, calms its eagerness, and causes it to look with joy to the gaining of the heights where perpetual sunshine reigns. Yes; God is now treating us as His children. He takes us by the hand, and conducts us over the bridge that spans the raging torrent. "When I was a child," says St. Paul, "I spoke as a child, I understood as a child, but when I became a man, I put away the things of a child." (1 Cor. xiii, 11).

NEED OF SELF-SACRIFICE

If we examine the advantages accruing from self-sacrifice we shall realise how necessary it is for acquiring charity. Passion often blinds the reason or rather presents a difficulty as a serious obstacle, and causes fear and falsehood to triumph. Now, self-sacrifice restrains such fears, for it presents in pleasing colours what previously appeared terrifying. It not only strengthens the will, but makes the body hardy to endure the rigours of the seasons. Who will say a soldier is not hardened even in his muscles by a severe and vigorous campaign? The Christian athlete not only becomes hardy, but has the satisfaction of knowing he is carrying out the exhortation of our Saviour: "If any man will come after Me, let him deny himself, and take up his cross daily and follow Me." (Luke ix, 23). Happiness will not be denied him; for he knows he is beginning to resemble Christ; he is commencing to live the life of Christ. Above all, he is pleasing the God he has learned to love, and every act of self-sacrifice binds him, like a hoop of steel, to the Infinite. And what a crown he is weaving for himself in heaven. Courage then, soldiers of Christ, think of your destiny, think of eternity. When St. Philip Neri was confronted with what demanded genuine self-sacrifice, he would rejoice, and casting his biretta in the air, exclaim: Paradise! Paradise!

But let us be practical; the important thing is to conquer what requires to be conquered; to withstand courageously attacks of sensuality, to give up daily some pleasures and satisfactions simply to please God, some too that may be quite lawful, but above all to have the courage to eradicate what should be eradicated.

A humorous incident is related of a boy, who was accustomed at supper to overcharge himself with food, and having asked for advice on the matter, was told to mortify himself. And so he did; he did not restrain himself from partaking of victuals but resolved never to open his mouth for five minutes after supper. Another boy being told of this cried out: that is no mortification; for Jones could not open his mouth after any meal.

We need discernment to practise self-sacrifice; we should break the net that holds the bird captive, and let the little songster go free to soar into the bright atmosphere, and to look down calmly on the turbulent world beneath.

We should avoid false mortifications. A musician will not tear his violin to shreds; no; he treats it sensitively, elicits music from its chords, and rejoices at the good results. So must we treat the body; we must remove from it all deleterious matter, then it will assist the soul, to sing the canticle of divine love.

These considerations teach us the necessity of a spiritual director. He will be our guide, our encourager, our restrainer, our light amid darkness. But he should be learned, pious and experienced. Prudence should crown his other gifts. Pay no attention to those who say they direct themselves. Very few really do so. When anything causes them trouble, they wisely ask for advice, and thus escape the danger of making serious mistakes.

EASY ACTS OF DIVINE LOVE

We are now in a position to profit by making easy acts of love. These consist in making short, but fervent ejaculations, which frequently repeated generate a habit that makes them sweet and attractive. There are many of these indulgenced by the Holy See: "Jesus my God, I love Thee above all things." (300 days); "O Heart of Jesus, burning with love for us, inflame our hearts with love of Thee." (500 days). The acts that spring spontaneously from the heart are best. Prayers for sinners, for the souls in Purgatory, the tempted, etc., are admirable acts of charity. Each day we might accustom ourselves to practise the corporal and spiritual works of mercy, among which are the following: to assist the needy, and the down-trodden, console those in grief, and relieve the suffering. In imitation of God's servants, we can visit the Blessed Sacrament, and also a statue of Our Blessed Lady. The love of God thrives on self-sacrifice; for every act of self-denial causes a flame to break forth that burns all that is opposed to God. Let us also ensure obtaining a reward for all we do, by making daily the good intention of performing everything to please God, to do all things out of love for God.

THOSE PROGRESSING

Those anxious to advance in divine love, and who are not? may at this time reach a crisis in cultivating the virtue of divine charity. They may find themselves attacked by *aridity*. But when this does not come from tepidity and with those anxious to love God it does not, it is decidedly an advance, and an important one, on the way we have chosen. In fact, it frequently happens this is the only way to advance. Take this example. You have often seen a child inclined to do what its mother does not wish. What does she do? She puts a liquid, not hurtful, but unpleasant, on the object the child desires to suck. The child, on perceiving the unpleasant taste, turns from it in disgust, and returns to it no more. So it is with sensible pleasure. We have been basking in its rays. The Lord wishes us to leave the paps of sensible delight, and partake of more substantial food. And so He withdraws sensible delights, and when we are faithful and generous, continuing our course in the midst of the aridity or dryness we undergo, He achieves His object.

It is well, however, not to allow the imagination to lead us to exaggerate this trial unduly. All experience it, and all can easily overcome it. The remedy is to persevere courageously at the work we find irksome. Every cloud has a silver lining, and very often the best part, which brings nourishment to men, animals and plants, is the dark part of the cloud.

The example of St. Anthony of the desert, the Father of the Monks, readily occurs to our minds, as an illustration of this point. When asked what were the greatest difficulties he had to encounter in acquiring the perfection of divine love, he answered: "The things I feared but which never happened." In these words there is much consolation to encourage the sincere.

There is no part of a Saint's life more interesting and none that bears more directly on the question of divine love than that which intervenes between the conversion and the attainment of the heights. And yet, very often no part of the written work is less developed than this. Frequently a few stray remarks are made to fill up the gap. In more recently written lives an attempt has been made to supply this defect, yet much remains to be done, before the ideal is attained. In many instances there are letters, diaries and notes; and if these were studied would afford much encouragement and consolation for those striving after divine love.

I call this a most important part of the person's career; for here it is that failure is more frequently found. St. Teresa says quite a number of people reach the prayer of quiet, but few go beyond it, because they are not prepared to make the sacrifices the perfection of charity demands. Were this part of the life analysed, we should find many faults revealed. We should certainly discover an inclination to abandon the difficult way, and impatience with self would often appear, yet there would also be disclosed a determination to persevere and win out, which nothing could conquer. Surely we must learn more about the way the candidate for sanctity conducted himself in the dark path, where great shadows were thrown across his way, where boulders threatened to dislodge and crash down upon him. What were his guides? Unerring faith; blind obedience; profound humility. These brought tranquillity of spirit, and gave him a glimpse of the heroic charity, where he would bask in the rays of perpetual sunshine.

If we are inclined to grow discouraged at this stage—and such a temptation is by no means uncommon—let us inspire ourselves with the following considerations: (1) that when previously inundated with delights, we desired, and even prayed perhaps to get an opportunity to do what would be most pleasing to God. We are getting it now, and all the more surely because we have not chosen it; (2) what we suffer is but a drop of water in the ocean compared with what our Divine Saviour endured on the cross. His agony was the result of His undying love for us, ours will be the result of our undying love for Him. When He is pleased to unite us with Himself on Calvary, the hill of lovers, surely we shall not refuse His invitation? (3) What we suffer now purifies our love as nothing else could.

LIGHT FROM SACRED SCRIPTURE

The Scriptures are replete with references to this state of
divine love. "The light of thy countenance, O Lord, is signed
upon us; thou hast given gladness in my heart." (Ps. iv, 7). The
light means the wonderful illuminations cast, especially by the
inspirations of the Holy Ghost, on the mysteries of our religion,
on the virtues we are to practise, but above all on our faults,
which when God reveals appear as a dark cloud intercept-
ing the rays of divine light. St. Paul says: "And this I pray that
your charity may more and more abound in knowledge, and all
understanding." (Phil. i, 9). If we are to love God as we should,
we must be enlightened regarding His perfections, beauty, simplicity, love, infinite goodness, etc., for how can we love God
if we know Him not? St. Stephen, standing before the Council
of the Jews could, when overwhelmed with the light of divine
illuminations, cry out: "Behold, I see the heavens opened and
the Son of Man standing on the right hand of God." (Acts vii,
55). Such a flood of light and grace penetrated his soul that like
another Paul, he seemed transported to the third heavens, and
there understood mysteries it was not given man to utter. Such
considerations urged the Apostle of the Gentiles, who never
allowed the lights he received to remain unfruitful, to exclaim:
"Brother, I do not count myself to have apprehended, but one
thing I do, forgetting the things that are behind, and stretching
forth myself to those that are before, I press towards the mark,
to the prize of the supernatural vocation of God in Christ
Jesus." (Philip iii, 13, 14). Living in so sinful a world as this,
and having such a propensity to evil, it is impossible, seeing the
devil is ever plotting against those of good will, to remain long
in the same position; we must either advance or go back.

Father Nieremberg[1] expresses some beautiful sentiments on
this subject. "We must use the things of this world no further

[1] Of Adoration in Spirit and Truth: p. 247.

than they conduce to the glory and love of God; they are only means, and are not to be used for themselves. . . . All will be vain and unprofitable, that does not conduct to God's glory. Can that profit a tree, which does not help to make it fruitful? What will it avail, if its leaves be gilded, its stock wrapped in silk, its boughs full of sparkling diamonds. All these will be to no purpose, and wholly unservicable; a little manure would be of greater consequence. All the treasures and riches of this world will afford no commodity unless they help us to glorify God." And we glorify Him especially by divine love.

MORE DIFFICULT ACTS

We can now advance to more difficult acts. We can with prudence exercise ourselves in zeal for the glory of God, and the salvation of souls. Zeal for souls is a direct result of divine charity, and when fervently carried out increases charity in the soul. But in this we shall meet with opposition, for the creature who is without sanctifying grace, and the devil who has deprived him of it, will fight strenuously to prevent his regaining it. To win souls to God, especially such as are abandoned, calls for a wholehearted exercise of divine love; for experience teaches that any work, where great graces are required, will not bear fruit, till nurtured by suffering, or self-sacrifice. Now self-sacrifice is the essential condition for acquiring the love of God; because self-love is the enemy of divine love, and self-sacrifice attacks it vigorously. Again, in ordinary affairs we shall be obliged to undergo little annoyances from others, and sometimes, perhaps without any apparent cause; a storm of opposition will be let loose against us. Did not the Saints meet with calumny and detraction? Yet they rejoiced in it, because they realised they were suffering for justice' sake: "Blessed are they that suffer persecution for justice' sake, for theirs is the kingdom of heaven." (Matt. v, 10). But we can rest assured God will not send us these till we are well prepared for them; for He always accommodates the burden to the back that has to carry it.

In all that we endure in the interests of divine love, we can always preserve calmness of spirit, and where we alone are concerned, can afford to ignore the ill-will, nay even the persecutions, of others. God always undertakes the cause of those, who, out of love for Him, and where there is no danger of scandal, refuse to defend themselves. St. Philip Neri used to follow in this the excellent principle, which some of us may find invaluable: "Despise being despised." Often we shall be confronted with the alternative of choosing between two courses of action, one of which is more pleasing to God than the other. In this matter each one must be left to his own discretion. The spirit of God breathes where it will; and what would be very useful for one, would be too severe for another. In this we should be guided by the prudent advice of a director. St. Teresa made a vow to do always the more perfect. I know a person who took a vow always to do what was more pleasing to God. But in both cases, I need hardly say, they had the approval of their directors.

In all this we should strive to cultivate a cheerful attitude. God loves a cheerful giver; and our lives are now tending towards the heights, and the heights are essentially cheerful. Sadness is not for us; it does not enter into our lives, unless to be summarily rejected. His gifts, even when trying, are the expression of His deep affection. As the rose, the fairest of flowers and emblem of charity, gives forth its sweetest perfume when cut and placed in a vase upon the altar, so shall we spread abroad the sweet odour of divine love, when we are sacrificed in His interests, and for the welfare of our neighbour.

THE PERFECT LOVERS OF GOD

Those who practise what has already been outlined will soon

reach union with God. This union of heart with heart, will with will, is perfect charity. This is exercised with a calm delight. The result is complete conformity with God's will. We shall have more to say in this subject in a later chapter. Here it will suffice to point out what St. Paul and St. Augustine teach on the subject:

"Be not conformed," says St. Paul, "to this world, but be reformed in the newness of your minds, that you may prove what is the good, and the acceptable, and the perfect will of God." (Rom. xii, 2). The Apostle here says let your minds, i.e., your souls, be renewed and restored by sanctifying grace to the form they had, when Adam lived in the garden of Eden and of course in the love of God.

St. Augustine[1] adds: "Now, therefore, the Apostle having exhorted us to give up our bodies a living sacrifice, pure and acceptable to God, our reasonable service, and not to be conformed to the world, but to be reformed in the newness of our minds that we might prove what is the good, acceptable and perfect will of God, that is to say, the true sacrifice of ourselves, adds: 'For I say by the grace that is given me to all that are among you, not to be more wise than it behoveth to be wise, but to be wise unto sobriety.' The will of God is *good*, when it prescribes what is to be done as in verses 2 and 3 of chapter xii of the Romans, *better*, when it tells you to forgive your enemies as it does in verses 9 to 16, and *perfect*, when it places before you Christian perfection, which consists in *perfect charity*, as in verses 16 to the end of the chapter (Rom. xii)."

This perfection results in perfect conformity with God's will, which is nothing else than the perfect love of God.

THE TWO WAYS

There are two ways pointed out by Jesus Christ Himself,

[1] De Civitate Dei. Lib. x, C.6.

by which we reach eternal life: the active and contemplative.

Richard of St. Victor[1] speaks of them as follows:

"Martha in one place labours with the body in respect of some things, but Mary by charity labours in many places as regards many things. For in contemplation and love of God she sees all things, has compassion on all, comprehends and embraces all. In comparison with her Martha may be said to be solicitous as regards a few things."

This is the story of Martha and Mary, as outlined in the Gospel, Martha being the ideal of the active, Mary of the contemplative life. One may question the ideal description here given by some writers and may ask: Did Our Lord intend the two ways to be so separated as Richard of Saint Victor has described? Scarcely, seeing they are perfectly united in Himself, and that He is our Model: "I am the way and the truth and life." (John xiv, 6). Besides, Our Lord does not condemn the way of Martha, He simply says she need not trouble herself in serving the guests who have visited her. Moreover, according to St. Luke (x, 38-42) who alone mentions this incident of Martha and Mary, Jesus said: Mary hath chosen the *good part* which shall not be taken from her, but as the words are placed in opposition to the serving of Martha, they are rightly translated as the *better part*. Yet it may be reasonably doubted if the two lives are ever completely separated; the active may, in the case of individual Saints, predominate over the contemplative, because they are better suited for it, as others are for the contemplative life. It is just to infer that St. Martha had much of the recollection of St. Mary Magdalen, and that St. Mary Magdalen was most exact in fulfilling her duties. It would be fatal to divorce the two ways, to remove the contemplative from the practice of virtue, or the practice of virtue and labour for souls from contemplation. St. Alphonsus states that the

[1] In Cant. 8.

success of active missionary life depends on the fire of charity that has been enkindled by contemplation. He also tells us of a man, who had reached the heights of contemplation, but neglecting the practice of humility, fell from his high estate, became a reprobate, lost the faith and died without giving any sign of repentance. Humility and obedience have always been considered the genuine tests of sanctity.

Still the upright will has nothing to fear. It can either by the active or contemplative way, or better by a combination of both, reach the heights of sanctity, i.e., of divine charity. There is a beautiful passage in St. Francis de Sales "Treatise on the Love of God,"[1] which I will quote here to encourage my readers:

"The indifferent heart is as a ball of wax in the hands of God, receiving with equal readiness all the impressions of the divine pleasure; it is a heart without choice, equally disposed for everything, having no other object of its will than the will of its God, and placing its affection not on the things that God wills, but on the will of God, Who wills them. Therefore, when God's will is in various things, it chooses at any cost that in which it most appears. God's will is found in marriage, and in virginity, but as it is more in virginity the indifferent heart makes choice of virginity though this cost it its life, as with St. Paul's dear daughter St. Thecla, with St. Cecily, St. Agatha and a thousand others. God's will is found in the service of the poor and of the rich, but yet somewhat more in serving the poor, and so the indifferent heart will choose that side. God's will lies in moderation amid consolations, and in patience amid tribulations; but the indifferent heart prefers the latter, as having more of God's will in it. To conclude, God's will is the sovereign object of the indifferent soul; wheresoever she sees it, she runs after the odour of its perfumes, directing her course ever thither where it most appears, without considering anything else. She

[1] Book ix, C.4.

is conducted by the divine will as by a beloved chain, which way soever it goes she follows."

We see then that union with God consists in conformity with God's will; and whether we go by the active way, or by the way of contemplation, that is the goal we must aim at. Let us do what is most sublime, if it be not the way God has designed for us, it is but utter waste of time.

Let us not imagine, however, that this state of the perfect love of God is beyond our reach; no, it is within the reach of all —priests, religious and lay-folk; for has not Our Lord said to all: "Be you therefore perfect, as also your heavenly Father is perfect." (Matt. v, 48)?

SANCTIFYING GRACE AND CHARITY

As we have so often heard that sanctifying grace and charity are always found together, that each removes the stain of grievous sin and merits heaven, an objection has, I presume, already suggested itself to the reader: Why have we the two? Would one of these, either sanctifying grace or charity, not suffice?

The answer is simple: Both are necessary.

The principle from which all the supernatural virtues spring is sanctifying grace, for it brings them into the soul, and with the aid of a motive revealed by faith and the assistance of actual grace, renders their acts meritorious of eternal life. Now the virtues are numerous, and are called into action as circumstances arise. For instance, if we suffer we are called to practise patience, when calumniated or insulted, we have to practise humility, if opposed by an enemy we have to cultivate charity, and if we have sinned, we must do penance. There is not an hour of the day but some virtue is demanded. *But this is not always charity.* Hence sanctifying grace, from which all the supernatural virtues spring, is always needed to give us the virtue we need to practise at a particular moment. But charity is also needed at all times; for it gives the *form*, soul, or life to all the other virtues, without it even faith and hope would be dead, and all the supernatural moral virtues would have vanished. Very frequently we are called to exercise it, but when it is not being practised it is ever ready, like a soldier on duty, to leap into the breach, present arms, and defend the castle of the soul.

THE MOTIVE THAT MOVES THE WILL

Motive is that which moves. With regard to the will, when there is question of its commanding the practice of a supernatural virtue, the motive must be some truth revealed by God.

The perfection of our love of God depends, to a great extent, on the motive by which we are influenced. I say *to a great extent* for the act also has its own objective perfection. In regard to charity the motive must be to love God for His own sake, and our neighbour as ourselves for God's sake; but in this there will be varying degrees of perfection.

The motives urging us to love God are very numerous, and when well pondered impel the will with overwhelming force. We shall consider them at some length in the following chapters. Here it will suffice to say that once God has created the will and revealed Himself as the Supreme Good, the will is obliged to love Him. But this is altogether for its own good; for there is no object more worthy of love, none that so ennobles the human soul as love of God. St. Augustine was ravished with delight at the thought that God, out of His infinite goodness, had commanded us to love Him. Were we compelled to serve Him as slaves this would be our due. But no, God desiring to share with us His infinite riches has made known how we are to profit by them. It is by uniting our wills to His will by divine love.

THE LOVE OF OUR NEIGHBOUR

The love by which we love God includes also that by which we love our neighbour. St. John has spoken clearly on the point. "If any man say I love God, and hateth his brother, he is a liar, for he that loveth not his brother whom he seeth, how can he love God, whom he seeth not?" (1st Ep. John, iv, 20). The two are so closely united that where the one is, there also is the other; for fraternal charity springs from the love of God.

Of course St. John is here speaking of supernatural love. St. Thomas asserts it is specifically the same act by which we love God, and love our neighbour. Cardinal Cajetan has wisely pointed out that we all, as God's children, are made to His image and likeness, created for His glory, redeemed by the Precious Blood of His Son, and destined, if we serve Him faithfully, to reign for ever in heaven. We thus participate in His gifts, are made by sanctifying grace partakers of the divine nature, and reflect, though in a very imperfect way, some perfection existing in God Himself. St. Teresa, treating of union with God, says there is nothing gives us greater security, and lets us know so clearly we are in the right way as the supernatural love of our neighbour.

CHAPTER III

God is Most Lovable

WE COME now to deal with the motives that urge us to love God. These will be included under two heads: the goodness of God to us, the goodness of God in Himself. Goodness diffuses itself, never tires of pouring out its gifts on others. And seeing that the evidence of divine goodness is found in everything, in the flowers of the field, the fruit on the trees, the birds that pour forth a melody of song, the rivers that run to the sea, the friends with whom we associate, the happiness that often inundates the human heart, we may rest assured we shall not look in vain, in creation, redemption and the sanctification of the soul, as well as the perfections of God Himself, for the strongest of motives to inflame our hearts with love. Now, it is these we are going to consider in the present chapter.

But first we must get a clear idea of what God is.

WHO IS GOD?

Several eminent authors have left us beautiful descriptions of what God is. That which I here select is from the Ven. Lessius, as it seems less abstract than the others.

"God," he says, "is infinite as the fruitful cause in which the whole range of being exists in a sublime degree. He embraces within Himself all the angelic mind, or even the divine mind, can conceive. Hence St. Gregory Nazianzen says: 'God is an immense ocean of being.' In Him are infinite worlds, and infinite species of angels, in Him are nations of peoples, and species of animals without end, there too are infinite species of colours, pictures, harmonies, etc. There are endless regions and cities,

endless plains and woods, and field and gardens, mountains and
fountains, rivers and seas, palaces and temples innumerable. In
truth all that is of value, beauty or splendour and delight, are
found in Him, and enjoyed in infinite abundance. For all these
things and infinite others besides, which no created mind can
conceive exist in the divine essence, wisdom and omnipotence,
in such a way that by one act of the will, He is able to create in
all abundance.

"He is infinite Majesty itself; for all kings and princes, nay
all the angels and blessed are His servants and slaves by nature,
though in His kindness and by the communication of His spirit,
He has adopted and called them by the name of children."[1]

St. Augustine, in his Confessions,[2] has given a magnificent
description of God, showing how He creates, supports, fills,
nourishes, overshadows and perfects all things.

St. Bernard, in his work on consideration (Book v, C.11,
12, 13), has with a masterly hand treated of the divine simplicity,
and deduced from it the endless perfections of the Almighty.

(A) GOD IS GOOD TO US
THE TEACHING OF OUR LORD

No one could teach us how infinitely lovable God is better
than Jesus Christ, seeing He is God. Has He not taught us to
call Him by the loving name of Father? Has he not in several
parables outlined the lovable characteristics of the Divine
Majesty?

Take the example of the Prodigal Son.

Our Lord takes care to indicate what would, in our eyes,
render God amiable and kind. He tells us a certain man had
two sons, one of whom, the elder, was faithful and obedient,
but the younger was a prodigal and spendthrift. The latter

[1] De Nominibus Divinis: C.3, 4, 9.
[2] Book i, C.4.

demanded his portion, i.e., the goods with which God had endowed him, and abandoning home, went forth and spent it all in riotous living. Soon all his goods were spent. He was ruined. And to preserve life, he had to turn to some useful employment, being compelled to herd swine. Crushed beneath the weight of his misery he exclaimed: "How many hired servants in my father's house abound with bread, and here I perish with hunger? I will arise from this state of degradation, and will go to my father, and say to him: Father I have sinned against heaven and before thee; I am not worthy to be called thy son, make me one of thy hired servants." (Luke xv, 17-19). And so he returns, but not without fear; for he knows his father may treat him as his sins deserve. Yet the father does not; when he beholds him he is delighted, goes forth to meet him, gives him the kiss of peace, brings forth the best robe, puts it on him, and makes a feast in his honour. Mark how every point that can win the heart of the sinner is emphasised by Jesus, and those points the severe and indignant would gladly dwell on, are concealed. He makes no reference to the scandal given, the disgrace brought on the family, the reparation and penance which justice itself demanded. No, he sees the good heart of his son, and is content. He knows well a display of mercy will afterwards develop all the reparation justice demands.

Now, suppose that young man had been your son, would you not have upbraided him with ingratitude, and have demanded immediate amends for the harm that had been done? Certainly you would. And what would have been the result? The young man disheartened by the severe treatment would have been embittered, and would have abandoned the home for ever. Too late, only when he had gone, would you have realised the serious mistake you had made.

Yet God acts with greater consideration. He does not, it is true, as the Good Shepherd afterwards does, go after him, and carry him back in triumph to the fold. No; he allows the Prodigal Son to fall low, and feed of the husks of swine, so that, becoming disgusted with his state, he may the more readily return.

God, who accomplishes all things here withdraws His graces to suit His ends. Evidently the father expected his return; for "When he was yet a great way off, his father saw him, and was moved with compassion, and running to him fell upon his neck and kissed him."

He does not state that the younger son supplanted in his father's affections the elder, though in the case of Jew and Gentile, which is here signified, that did happen. God is most compassionate: He drives no one to desperation; He would win all, and He simply says to the elder brother, who is disgruntled at what has happened: "Thou are always with me and all I have is thine."

Whether we apply the parable, as is generally done, to the Gentiles who for thousands of years had abandoned their Father's house, or to the repenting sinner, the lesson is the same. How lovable is God, and how amiable are His ways! No sooner has the Gospel been preached than people abandon sin, and commence to serve their God, and marvellous examples of heroic virtue begin to flourish in the garden of the Church. Consider the results: the virgins, who have died in defence of faith and charity; the confessors, who have preached the Gospel with such marvellous success; the martyrs, who by their blood have glorified the Church, and have shown us how to walk in the blood-stained footsteps of our divine Master, and so many others, widows, married men and women, as well as children who have given us inspiring examples of patience.

THE MOTIVE ITSELF

Before dealing directly with Creation, Redemption and Sanctification, we must state that if we are to have the virtue of charity in our souls it must be infused by God; if we are to practise its acts, we must have a supernatural motive, i.e., a truth revealed by God that moves the will. In the next place this truth must deal with some aspect of the divine goodness, either His goodness to us, or His goodness in itself, for the will, which is the faculty that exercises charity, is drawn only by the good. And thirdly it must be exercised under the influence of grace, e.g., a soul in the state of grace has power to elicit a supernatural, a charitable act, but requires actual grace to produce that act; but a soul in the state of grievous sin will require a special actual grace to supply what corresponds to the power, and also to bestow what is needed to bring about the act. For a soul in mortal sin can make an act of charity, and that act, produced as we have described, will bring into the soul the state of sanctifying grace.

THE GOODNESS OF THE FATHER, SON AND HOLY GHOST

If we are to grasp more clearly the infinite goodness of God, we must consider Him in Creation, Redemption, and Sanctification. In the creation of the human race we consider God, the Father, for creation, being a work of infinite power, is specially attributed to Him; in Redemption we consider the Son, for He has redeemed us; in Sanctification we consider the Holy Ghost, for as it is a work of divine love, it is particularly assigned to Him.

CREATION

Of the innumerable persons whom God could have created, and who, perhaps, would have served Him better than we, God has been pleased to choose us. It has been said by some that what is wonderful in creation is not that God has chosen this or that person, but that He has created at all. For creation is

an all-powerful act, demanding the work of a self-existing Being.
Still, in the fact that God has made the special choice of certain
people, there is a specific preference, that makes a strong appeal
to the individual chosen. It is on this point we here insist. He
has drawn us out of nothing, not because of any merits on our
part, but simply because of His infinite goodness, and has made
us images of Himself. Adam and Eve were created in the state
of sanctifying grace but when they fell the whole race was sunk
in the corruption of death. But then God re-created us. He
immediately promised a Redeemer, Who would save the people
from their sins. And who was He? No other than God Himself
—the Second Person of the Blessed Trinity. (Gen. iii, 15).
And why did He come Himself? Because God being a zealous
Lover will have no one come between Himself and the hearts
that love Him. What wisdom is displayed in this act of God!
Had He sent an angel to redeem us, our affections would have
been divided between the angel and God. And as He makes it
clear that we must give Him our whole hearts, so He has given
His whole Heart to us. He says: "My son, give Me thy heart;
and let thy eyes keep My ways." (Prov. xxiii, 26). And Our
Lord tells us! "Thou shalt love the Lord thy God with thy
whole heart." (Matt. xxii, 37). He says: "All I have is thine."
(Luke xv, 31).

God, Who is a jealous lover, would have our hearts for
Himself. Yet this jealousy on the part of God is entirely for
our good. It is to withdraw our affections from things of earth,
and centre them on Him, draw them from riches, honours,
pleasures, passions, the passing beauty of the creature, from our
own self-love, our vain desires—all of which are so absorbing,
and which so enthral the heart. When we have done this, we
shall place all our affections in God, and finding them inflamed
with the fire of divine love, shall experience little difficulty in
making our acts correspond with them.

But there is jealousy also in the heart of the lover. It is to give all its love to God, and at the same time draw all hearts to Him. Indeed, such a soul would, did it lie in her power, inflame the entire world with love for God, and is therefore green with jealousy when she sees contemptible objects occupy the throne of men's hearts that should be reserved for the Almighty alone.

There are three extraordinary elements in the design of creation, which point out the infinite wisdom and goodness of God, but which, if we did not understand properly, might lead us to imagine that in some of these God did not manifest His accustomed mercy, kindness and lovableness.

The first is that God chose a certain race, kept it apart from the rest of the world since the days of Abraham, and did not send the Redeemer till thousands of years after the Fall of Adam.

The fact that God chose a race apart, and kept it separated, ensured that the types and prophecies which so perfectly represented the Redeemer, and so clearly proved He was God, had an opportunity to develop, since the Jewish race had the true religion and could be used as a medium to foreshadow the good things to come. Moreover, had God come to redeem mankind, when Adam fell, men would not have appreciated the gift they received, but would have despised, as Adam and Eve had already done, the infinite blessing of the Beatific Vision. This shows the goodness of God.

In the second place God allowed mankind to descend into the depths of depravity. It required thousands of years to let men reach the depths to which crime and immorality could drag them, and teach them their weakness and nothingness, when bereft of the abundant assistance of divine grace. True, they always received sufficient grace, for the Passion of Christ produced its effects before and after the Sacrifice of Calvary, but these merely sufficient graces did not, unless people rendered them efficacious by prayer, produce the necessary results. This object lesson has not been lost on the world, for when God did take men and women from the off-scourings of the earth, and make them angels of purity, and seraphs of love, the world stood in amazement at the spectacle.

In the third place, amid this maelstrom of spiritual ruin, one creature, Mary the Mother of God, was preserved intact from the prevailing corruption.

And what a blessing it was that God so preserved her, for she was worthy to be the Mother of the Redeemer, worthy to be our Model in regard to that charity, which man had so barbarously outraged and worthy to assist us by the help she could always obtain from God. The creation of Mary was, in the divine design, an act of great love. It was not due mankind. It was purchased for her and for us only by the merits of the Precious Blood of Jesus. All these prove how good God has been to us.

REDEMPTION

Our Lord becomes a child. What could inspire greater love in our hearts than to see the infinite God of heaven and earth become a little Babe for our sake. This divine Child does not accuse us of our sins, does not frighten us with thunder and lightning, as God once did with the Jews on Mount Sinai; no, He stretches out His hands to inspire compassion, sympathy and love. When we see Him announced by the angels and adored by the shepherds, our faith is enlivened, and our charity inflamed. When the Wise Men offer their gifts of gold, frankincense and myrrh, our hearts are moved with joy, and then His Godhead, Priesthood and Humanity compel us to pay Him the homage He deserves. "The charity of Christ presses us . . . But all things are of God, who hath reconciled us to Himself by Christ, and hath given us the ministry of reconciliation. For God indeed

was in Christ reconciling the world to Himself, not imputing
to them their sins." (II Cor. v, 14, 18, 19).

In the next place, if we consider the gifts bestowed on men
by God in redeeming us, we shall be convinced that God is
most lovable. He has given us an infinite gift in bestowing
Himself; in fact, He has given us all. St. Paul, writing to Titus,
does not hesitate to say that Jesus is the embodiment of all
kindness and goodness; since He has come "that He might
redeem us from all iniquity, and might cleanse to Himself a
people acceptable, a pursuer of good works." (Tit. ii, 11, 14
and iii, 4). And in our pursuing good works, He does not ask
us to do anything He has not done Himself, in truth He demands
a great deal less.

Be assured it would require an infinite mind to probe the
depths of love concealed in the mystery of the Incarnation.
When the angels fell, God did not redeem them by assuming
their nature; He justly condemned the rebellious hosts to hell.
But when man fell He promised and ultimately sent a Redeemer.
Let us dwell briefly on the promise of the divine Redeemer,
made by God in the Garden of Eden, and we shall see how He
so acted as to draw all hearts to Himself. "I will put enmities
between thee and the woman, between thy seed and her seed,
she (or he) shall crush thy head, and thou shalt lie in wait for
her heel." (Gen. iii, 15). The woman, of whom there is question here is certainly not Eve, for Satan has just succeeded
in crushing her head, and she is punished more severely than
Adam, because more guilty. Moreover, she is the mother of all
the living. She is not the mother of some in contrast with others
who belong to Satan. But it is the *woman* above all others, who
was conceived Immaculate, and who during her whole life never
committed the slightest fault, Mary with the divine Child in her
arms, crushing the serpent's head. It matters not in the least
whether we read He or She shall crush thy head, because it is

the Child, who as God, has infinite power, with His Mother, that does it. This woman, as being the Mother of the Redeemer, becomes Mother of those whom Christ redeemed. She is a tender and compassionate Mother, deeply interested in our spiritual welfare, always willing to pray for us, if we pray to her.

We have been redeemed at a great price, and for those determined to make a good use of Redemption, the appreciation of its value will be immensely increased. Christ foresaw who would profit by His Passion and Death, and when He was on the Cross, these consoled His aching Heart. He died, indeed, for each of us as if there were no other in the world to die for. For His merits, being those of God, are infinite, so the satisfaction He makes must also be of infinite value, and therefore, however much one partakes of these merits, they always remain infinite for the others.

And why do I make so little return for all He has done? It arises from want of generosity in love. Were a man of the world to do for me one hundredth part of all that Christ has done, I should never forget it, and if I did, the whole world would justly call me an ungrateful wretch. But when there is question of forgetting God, and not making a suitable return, the world does not condemn but applauds. What inconsistency!

The blessings we have received through Jesus Christ were not unknown to the prophet Isaias. Contemplating them he cried out: "God is my Saviour, I will deal confidently and will not fear; because the Lord is my strength and my praise, and He is become my salvation. You shall draw waters with joy out of the Saviour's fountains." (Is. xii, 2, 3). As we shall have occasion later to consider at some length the Passion of Our Lord, as a motive for inflaming us with love, we shall merely state here that the sufferings endured by Jesus must be the delight of the Blessed in heaven, and the envy of the demons in hell; and all must be in consternation at the fact that men treat their Creator and Redeemer not as their best Friend, but as their greatest enemy.

SANCTIFICATION

We must now consider the goodness and lovableness of God in sanctifying our souls. For this purpose He sent the Holy Ghost, as Comforter and Sanctifier. "But the Paraclete, the Holy Ghost, whom the Father will send in My name, He will teach you all things, and bring all things to your mind, whatsoever I shall have said to you." (John xiv, 26). And what a stupendous work the Holy Ghost accomplishes in the perfecting of souls! His patience is untiring, His kindness inexhaustible, His zeal unquenchable. Often has He raised souls to extraordinary heights, bestowing on them the gift of prayer, advancing them from virtue to virtue, and at length introducing them to the contemplation of His infinite perfections, when, because of some sensual attraction, some vile trifle, they have cast prayer to the winds, trampled on the gifts that were bestowed, and plunged headlong into the mire of immorality. And yet were such souls to repent, the Holy Ghost would commence the work of their sanctification over again and advance them into new and fertile regions, where He would make use of their humility and experience to ensure the coveted victory.

The coveted victory! Ah! what victories are daily gained in the interior life of our souls by the Holy Spirit, victories hidden from the world, but appreciated in heaven. A dying sinner is snatched from the jaws of hell, that are yawning to devour him; victims to evil, hear sermons, are interiorly moved, resolve to amend, and lo! like brands snatched from the burning, are planted near the living waters, develop into beautiful specimens, and produce fruit in abundance. Perhaps, a Christian is insulted, his nature rebels at the outrage, immediately divine grace asserts itself, revealing to him the meek and humble Jesus, and he resolves to follow the Divine Exemplar. But not without a struggle. The insult stings his heart, the thought of what people will say, if he takes the matter quietly, annoys him. Still he struggles manfully, and then a citadel of self-love is taken, joy is given to the angels, and often edification to men.

In addition to this the Holy Ghost provides us with an excellent, an infallible guide in the Catholic Church. There are teaching institutions in abundance to train the mind and heart. There are priests—many priests—to assist us by their instructions and example.

And what models for us to follow has the Holy Spirit raised up? There are men and women who have been infallibly declared our models in the work of sanctification. They grace every path of life; they are capable of inspiring every class of people. Such are St. Francis of Assisi, St. John of God, St. Philip Neri, St. Francis de Sales, and St. Alphonsus among men and St. Monica, St. Gertrude, St. Catherine of Siena, St. Teresa, St. Margaret Mary, St. Gemma Galgani, and the Little Flower of Jesus, among women, all of whom are the direct result of the delicate training undertaken by the Holy Ghost. It has been wisely stated that the work of sanctifying a soul, as undertaken by God, is even greater than that of creating it; for in the latter case God acts independently of the human will, and is not hampered by it, but in the former instance only too often do the stubborn wills of man destroy everything. And yet the Holy Ghost never over-rides freedom of the will, but by the calmness of interior remorse bestowed on the wayward, by the sweetness of attractions given the fervent, He draws all nearer Himself, and advances them in the ways of divine love.

OTHER MOTIVES

Many other supernatural motives, revealing the goodness of God to us might be dwelt on; indeed, so many are they it would be very difficult to exhaust them all. In individual cases, there may have been preservation from sin, the bestowal of a religious vocation, or of a vocation to the Priesthood, all of which being manifest indications of God's goodness, inspire man with an increase of love. What has been said here will suggest other motives that, when divine charity is tried, will uphold us in the combat.

Merely natural motives, however, are not sufficient to produce acts of charity. They do not call the infused virtue into operation. But frequently what in the case of good Catholics appear merely natural acts are, in reality, acts of charity, for they spring from gratitude to God, and zeal for His glory.

(b) GOD AS GOOD IN HIMSELF

We now approach a subject that has always been the delight of the Saints: the fact that God is good and perfect in Himself.

In the material world there is an endless amount of perfection. We behold it in the beauty of the fields, in the majesty of the trees, in the power of the river and the ocean, in the plumage of the birds, in the graceful forms of animals, in sapphires and gems of every hue, in the gold and silver dug out of the mines, in the charm, the cleverness, the universality of man. All these remind us of the infinite perfections of God, in Whom they exist in a sublime degree, seeing He has created them. Since only an infinite, self-existing Being can create, all that I have mentioned and an infinite amount more of beauty, perfection, goodness, must be in God in an eminent way.

But what has divine perfection to do with God's goodness in Himself? Much, because the divine perfections when considered as desirable to the will constitute the divine goodness. And since God is infinitely perfect, and since these perfections are most lovable, most desirable, God is infinitely good. We can well understand how the divine will loves what is infinitely perfect, because He loves Himself with an infinite love. But how can man do so? By being united to God. And he is united by charity: "Jesus answered and said to him: if any man love me, he will keep my word. And my Father will love him, and we will come to him and make our abode with him." (John xiv, 23).

THE SCRIPTURES TELL US GOD IS INFINITELY GOOD AND PERFECT

When Moses was commissioned to lead the chosen people out of Egypt, he asked God to tell him who was sending him, so that he might tell the Jews, when they asked him; "Lo, I shall go to the children of Israel and say to them: the God of your fathers has sent me to you. If they should say to me: what is his name? what shall I say to them?"

God answered Moses, saying: "I am Who am." He said: "Thus shalt thou say to the children of Israel: *He Who is hath sent me.*" (Exod. iii, 13, 14). In these four words: "I am Who am" we find briefly stated all that is needed to inform us of the infinite goodness of God. "I am Who am" means I am the one Who exists of Himself, Who depends on nothing, but on Whom all else depends; in Whom there is neither weakness, nor imperfection, but all goodness. Nothing imperfect, not even what might exist in thought, could be attributed to God.

Here Moses has asked God His name; God tells him. Now, by name is meant what a person is, and what his individualising qualities are. In respect of God this is His self-existence. God is self-subsisting, and He alone is this. This being so, God is perfect, and is infinitely good. Because of this He is the same yesterday, to-day and for ever. There is no past with Him; there can be no future; there is only the present. The creation of the world did not change Him; even when the Second Person of the Blessed Trinity assumed human nature, it effected no *real* change. Why? Because He is infinite in every perfection, and nothing could be added to Him.

God is *immense*. He fills all space, and would fill a greater did such exist. He is *eternal*. This is difficult for us to grasp; but when we realise He never had a past, never can have a future, but exists in the *"now"* of eternity, it becomes much easier to apprehend. He is *one*: it would be impossible for us to think of any God existing but the one true God. He is infinitely *pure*, *wise*, *holy*, *merciful*, *just* and *loving*. All that could be conceived, and an endless amount more we cannot imagine, exist in God, *making Him most lovable*; for God, being infinitely perfect, is the Supreme Good, deserving of an infinite love.

While we read these words, we shall very probably desire to make acts of love to the Supreme Good, telling Him how we would love Him and would make Him loved by others. We would as He deserves make Him loved by the whole world. Such acts satisfy the soul, and do not interrupt the thread of the narrative.

TWO COMPARISONS

We shall now give two comparisons, which will assist us in grasping what the infinitely good God is.

In the first place we take the example of a painter, representing a very beautiful image on a canvas. He commences by drawing an outline of the idea he has in his mind, then by degrees fills in the lines, shades and colouring, that make it as realistic as possible. So when we speak of God, we attribute to Him all that is good, all that is perfect in the world. We attribute to Him truth, wisdom and power, and we do so in their proper meaning, for in the idea of these there is no imperfection. But in addition to these we ascribe to God speech, hearing, etc., since these do imply perfection; but we can attribute them to God only in a sublime sense, i.e., with all imperfection removed. But as all these in the creature are in a restricted, but in God in an infinitely perfect, sense they must be all attributed to Him in an *eminent* form. And as we perfect the painting by developing all the lines that bring out the mind, the nobility, the beauty and character of the individual, so we develop in our minds the majesty, splendour and glory of the Trinity in God. In the next place we take the example of a sculptor, chiselling from a piece of marble the image of a man. This he does by striking very small pieces from the slab, till at length the image of the person begins to appear. In the end it almost appears as a living reflection of the original and when executed by a master-hand gives a much more perfect image than the painting. For in it we have matter and form, i.e., substance, representing the one who has been sculptured, and with a little imagination we could visualise the original. But when the statue is painted, we have in it as perfect an image as could be wrought. The colour on the cheeks, the shade of the garments, the eyes, blue, brown or grey, as the case may be, together with a thousand other traits, give the whole a realistic appearance. All the statue now needs is life to make it practically the original. In thinking of God then, when we attribute to Him in a sublime sense all goodness, and deny Him all imperfection, we have as perfect an image as could be desired, not absolutely so, of course, for the finite mind can never hope to conceive an adequate idea of the infinite.

What a sublime idea had St. Augustine, St. Bernard, St. Thomas and St. Alphonsus of God! They not only studied what those who had gone before wrote of Him, but they had infused knowledge, which elevated their ideas above all we can imagine. One has only to read St. Bernard telling us of the greatness, the depth, the simplicity, the eternity of God to see how sublime are his thoughts of God compared with those of ordinary people. A description such as this leaves a deep impression on the thinking people of all time.

LOVE BETWEEN FATHER, SON AND HOLY GHOST

If we wish to grasp more clearly the infinite goodness of God, we must consider the love the Father, Son and Holy Ghost have for each other.

The Catholic Church teaches that between the Eternal Father and the Divine Son there exists from all eternity an infinite love. It is mutual, and from it proceeds the Holy Ghost, Who is divine love itself. The sufferings endured on this earth by the Word Incarnate were the expression of that eternal love. The Eternal Father, while accepting the offering of His Son, for it satisfied perfectly the demands of divine justice, had the greatest sympathy for Him in His sufferings. How lovable then must God be in Himself! There is no other love such as this in the whole range of being; nay, any love among creatures is but an image of that between the Father, Son and Holy Ghost. It is not so much that God has love, as that God is love; for as St. Augustine has wisely stated, all that we can say God has, that He is. But what will appeal in a special way to each one is that we as God's creatures, as souls redeemed, as souls sanctified, are in some way included in this divine love of Father, Son and Holy Ghost. One has but to read the discourse of Our Lord at His Last Supper, as given by St. John, to learn how the Eternal Father, the Divine Son, the Holy Ghost, love those who love God.

GOD IN PARADISE

We can never hope to grasp fully how lovable God is till we ascend into heaven, and there see Him face to face. In the meantime let us in spirit ascend into the abode of eternal bliss, and there contemplate the Object of the love of the Blessed. We shall dwell first on the Sacred Heart, next on Mary Immaculate, then on the choirs of angels, and lastly on the entrancing spectacle of the Saints.

The Sacred Heart of all the hearts of existing things, has alone given God the love that is worthy of Him. Blessed Colombière, the director of St. Margaret Mary, has asserted: "The principal virtue we claim to honour in it (the Sacred Heart) is first a most ardent love of the Eternal Father." In this Heart there is the love of the Second Person of the Adorable Trinity, which is uncreated love, and there is also the created love proper to Christ as perfect man, and worthy to be united in His human nature to the Person of the Godhead. The love of the Sacred Heart is a fire, the heat of which surpasses all that can be imagined. St. Margaret Mary beheld on one occasion the Sacred Heart so inflamed with love that she was surprised it did not consume the whole world.

But the Sacred Heart has not only an undying love for the Eternal Father, It also has a most ardent love for us. To St. Gertrude Our Lord revealed He had reserved this devotion for these latter ages of the world to awaken faith in the minds, and inflame love in the hearts of men. This Heart in heaven is ever making intercession for us, and obtaining pardon for sin. Our Lord said to St. Margaret Mary: "Behold this heart which has so loved men, that it has spared nothing even to being exhausted and consumed for them."

"The love of Jesus for man is not separated and apart from His love of His Eternal Father; for in that love its love for man finds its source and motive, and with that love it is wholly permeated."[1] No one ever fulfilled the commandment thou shalt love the Lord thy God as Jesus did, and no one ever

[1] Bainvel: Devotion to the Sacred Heart: p. 91 (Lond. 1925).

fulfilled its counterpart, thou shalt love thy neighbour as thyself, with such perfection. Some seem to imagine that the love of God in the heart of man is in some unaccountable way incompatible with his human love. So far is this from the truth that we can say that without a genuine love of God there cannot be a pure and unselfish love of man in the hearts of God's creatures.

From what has been said here, two lessons can be learned: The infinite love the Sacred Heart has for the Eternal Father, and therefore how infinitely lovable God must be in Himself, and in the next place how we should, after the model of the Sacred Heart learn to love God with our whole souls.

OUR BLESSED LADY

Next to the Heart of Jesus, no heart ever loved God as did the Immaculate Heart of Mary. Of all creatures she alone fulfilled, according to the perfection a creature can attain, the command to love God with the whole heart, the whole soul, with all the strength, and with all the mind. God, as He knew Mary would be His Mother, and the Queen of angels and saints, fashioned her heart specially to love Him with a pure, a perfect, an heroic love.

Mary recognised her privileges and graces and thanked God for them. Never did she allow an opportunity of serving Him perfectly to pass unnoticed. And love was the guiding principle that rendered her life so perfect.

How does she love God now in heaven? With all the powers of soul and body. Her one desire is to love Him perfectly, and see Him so loved by others. St. Alphonsus says it is her privilege to go around and distribute a sweet liquid, which is nothing but the love of God.

The fact that God has so created Mary, as we have delineated in this section, shows how infinitely good He is in Himself, and how kind He is to His creatures.

THE ANGELS AND SAINTS IN THEIR LOVE OF GOD

This is a subject on which very much could be written; indeed, we could never hope to exhaust the subject.

The angels, unlike men and women on this earth, can love God with all the force and power of their natures, because they are not handicapped by the matter that individualises. They are pure spirits, having bright intellects and strong wills, and each of them is a species in himself. They are divided into choirs, and one of them the highest, the Seraphim, is, by their office, specially devoted to honouring God by the love they bear Him. These are balls of fire; and they are privileged to love God to the uttermost power of their being.

And what shall we say of the Saints? On this earth, they sought their salvation, yea, their sanctification in practising conformity with God's will. Now in heaven they love Him with such uniformity that their wills are one with His. These are the models we are invited to imitate.

HOW MEN AND WOMEN HAVE LOVED GOD

The mind of man, though it has a wonderful capacity for acquiring and increasing knowledge, yet (especially in the beginning of life) does so slowly and with much difficulty. But if men and women lack brilliancy of intellect—and in many instances they do—they have something more valuable, they have marvellous powers of loving. They can love with all the force of their nature, and this love when directed to God can be increased by the desires they cherish. Now, man's desires can embrace the infinite, he can desire to love God as much as

He deserves to be loved, and God is pleased with such desires and rewards them abundantly. Man also can unite his love with the love of the Sacred Heart, and can in this way love the Supreme Good as much as It wishes to be loved. An example will make this clear, and at the same time show how wonderful is the innate power of the heart of man to love. We read in the life of St. Mary Magdalen de Pazzi that she had a remarkable vision of the angelic youth, St. Aloysius, in Paradise. She beheld him shining with such splendour in heaven that his glory seemed to equal that of even the great Saints. She was surprised that one who died so young could have attained such merits, and she begged God to enlighten her as to its cause. She received the following answer. Aloysius, like the Prophet Daniel, was a man of desires, he longed to love God as much as He deserved to be loved; but since that was impossible the fervour of the ardent desires he cherished, and which he could not satisfy, caused his death.

We shall turn now to consider how some of the Saints have loved God. The examples I shall choose are few, yet there is scarcely a Saint in the calendar but was equally ravished with divine love.

We see the heart of St. Augustine inflamed with such a consuming fire of love that it produced those marvellous books, which have been the wonder of the world since his own day. We behold the spectacle of St. Bernard, explaining the song of love, and pouring forth from his heart those streams of fire that enraptured the hearts of his hearers. We gaze with admiration on St. Catherine of Siena, uniting the active to the passive life, practising a high degree of virtue and of contemplation, spending herself and being spent in the interests of the Church, whose visible Head she desired to lead back to Rome. We have heard of the heart of St. Teresa, that was transfixed with the dart of a Seraph, under which she swooned from the attack of pain and joy. She received this gift from God, because of her ardent love of Him. We have read that the heart of St. Philip Neri, through the fervour of his love, increased to twice its normal size, and broke two of his ribs.

DEEDS STRONGER THAN WORDS

But deeds are stronger than words, a truth which urged St. John to say: "Let us love not in word nor in tongue, but in deed and in truth." (1 John iii, 18). What shall we say of so many missioners, who like St. Alphonsus have endured cold, hunger, suffering and contempt to raise the weak and ignorant from sin, and make them lovers of the Crucified? Who could estimate the deep love that burned in the heart of St. Francis de Sales, who stated that if he knew there was a chord in his heart that did not vibrate with the love of God, he would instantly pluck it out? How much love for God did he manifest during his missionary activities in the Chablais, where he converted 70,000 souls! What self-sacrifice did he exercise as a Bishop? What zeal did he show by founding the Order of the Visitation for those of his penitents who were unable to endure the more severe rigours of Carmel! Who could hope to reckon the ardour of St. Peter of Alcantara, who to please God lived in the direst poverty, undertook heroic labours for the salvation of souls, and at the same time reformed his Order? Benedict the Fourteenth has said of St. Teresa that her conduct in founding so many convents, where God would be worthily served, clearly indicated her heroic faith. St. Agnes at the age of thirteen, when the world fawned on her, despised it all, and laid down her life in defence of her virginity. Such examples, and thousands of others, stand out prominently in the history of the Church, warning us not to give our hearts to creatures, but to keep them pure and undefiled in union with the God of heaven. All these people are on fire, burning like the Seraphim, and jealous because all the world does not love God as they do.

We can, then, without any fear of contradiction, assert that if the Sacred Passion of Our Lord had effected no other results than those enumerated here, it would have to be reckoned as a marvellous success. But, indeed, it has produced other wonders, and all of them compel our admiration. What is here recorded is but a fraction of the victories it has won.

St. John in the Apocalypse, relating the visions with which he was regaled in Patmos, beheld so many victories that they would baffle description. Speaking of those whom he saw in Paradise, he said: "I saw a great multitude, which no man could number, of all nations, and tribes, and peoples, and tongues, standing before the throne, and in the sight of the Lamb, clothed with white robes and palms in their hands." (Apoc. vii, 9). We may not be able to emulate the heroism of the Saints, but we can at least admire them, and follow them at a distance. Above all we can desire to love God as they did, and since our desires may be endless, we can by them embrace the infinite.

PRAYER

We shall conclude this chapter with the following prayer, asking God for a pure love of Himself:

O God, Lover of all mankind, Who takest delight in the simple and pure of heart, come into my soul, and grant that I become enamoured of Thee. As the Jews, travelling to the Promised Land were guided by the fire that burned brightly in the darkest night, so may I by the light and fire of Thy divine Presence pass through the darkness of this life, and reach the love of eternity, through Christ, Our Lord. Amen.

The Passion & Death of Christ

CHAPTER IV

St. Alphonsus is of opinion that there is no stronger motive to nourish divine love in our hearts than the Passion and Death of Jesus Christ. For every wound of His is a tongue declaring the infinite love He bore us, and how He desires to be loved in return. When we behold such a display of devotion, we are compelled to make a return of affection.

The present writer has, from the view-point of faith[1] already dealt with this subject, and therefore treats it here only in so far as it refers to divine love.

THE CONNECTION BETWEEN SUFFERING AND LOVE

The reader will naturally expect here, where we deal with the exquisite sufferings of Our Lord, an explanation of the connection between suffering and love. The close relation existing between the two is so often repeated in spiritual books that we only too often find it taken for granted. This, however, is not as it should be.

Suffering strengthens love. This scarcely needs proof; for we have practical experience of it daily. Of all her children, who is the one the mother loves most? That one that has cost her most suffering. The child may be sickly, weak and deformed, yet the mother will sacrifice all she has to save its life. She beholds in the little one lovable qualities hidden from every eye but her own.

[1] In *I Believe in God*, C. V. pp. 50-63. Published Browne and Nolan, Dublin.

I remember going with another priest to visit a family that had need of our assistance. In the home we saw only the mother and her deformed child. The child unfortunately had little to attract the affections of anyone, still the poor mother had a tender devotion towards him. Its misery awakened her sympathy; the neglect it suffered at the hands of the world had won her whole-hearted affection. We were both struck by this, and my companion dwelt fondly on the fact that the helpless child had gained all the love of its mother. And just as well it did; for it could scarcely find another friend in the world. Something similar must be at the root of the devotion shown us by Jesus and Mary, for our redemption has cost them so much, and our sanctification has demanded a great sacrifice.

Suffering, in the next place, is the cost of love. So strong is this instinct that we frequently see a person prove another's love by what is termed the acid test of suffering. No surer means could be discovered to find out how genuine is the love one bears another.

Suffering is also the means by which love perseveres. Friendship is begun in favours, but is consummated in suffering. No one could understand this better than God, and it is the way He takes to perfect friendship. Besides, love lives on sacrifice; now genuine self-sacrifice consists in suffering.

Who can doubt then that suffering and love are very closely connected, so much so that, generally speaking, one is the counterpart of the other?

SUFFERINGS OF JESUS ON THE CROSS

In this chapter we shall confine our attention to the sufferings Our Lord endured on the Cross.

The Prophet Isaias assures us that when Our Redeemer was nailed to the Cross there was not, from the crown of His head to the sole of His feet, any part whole in Him. "Surely he hath borne our infirmities, and carried our sorrows, and we have thought him as it were a leper and as one struck by God and afflicted. But he was wounded for our iniquities, and he was bruised for our sins; the chastisement of our peace was upon him. And by his bruises we are healed." (Is. liii, 4, 5). Our Lord, after being nailed, was raised on the cross. This agony was excruciating in the extreme; yet strange as it may seem it was to this Jesus looked forward as the all-powerful means of drawing all hearts to Himself: "And I, if I be lifted up, will draw all things to myself." (John xii, 32). The exaltation of the Cross, celebrated by the Church on September the 14th. is a great feast, marking the beginning of the Little Lent, observed in some Contemplative Orders. Though the feast specially commemorates the recovery by Heraclius (629 A.D.) of the true cross from the Persians, and its exaltation by him on Mount Calvary, yet it also includes the exaltation of the cross, on which Jesus was hanging after the nailing had taken place. This was in reality the beginning of man's freedom from spiritual slavery, and as such the feast is celebrated.

The crown of thorns, which is on the head of Jesus, covers the entire head as with a helmet. The Jews had the reputation of being experts in plaiting a crown of this kind, so as to cause exquisite suffering and deep humiliation. As the head is the centre of the nerves of the body, and as a well-formed head adds dignity to the whole person, we can see clearly how this instrument of torture inflicted not only suffering, but humiliation. It certainly caused some of the most intense pains endured during the Passion; for it was worn not only when He carried the cross, but when He was on the cross, and prevented Him from placing His head against the cross to alleviate the suffering endured. Besides, it was several times removed, and as often replaced. But the crown was not merely placed on the head, it was pressed down and its sharp thorns driven with an instrument into the skull. The Ven. Thomas of Jesus states that these pierced so deeply as to re-appear above the eyes. When this occurred streams of blood gushed from the perforations, and ran down His face, so that the sacred countenance of Jesus, which had been the delight of angels and men, was disfigured beyond recognition. Now as He lies on the cross drops of blood slowly ooze from the wounds these thorns have made.

And why was Our Lord pleased to endure such dreadful agony? To make atonement for the sins of thought, among which were uncharitable thoughts, which were violations of His own Commandment. Never in the history of the world has thought run riot as it has to-day; for it has rebelled fiercely against truth, and plunged into a whirlpool of error. It would be difficult to find a parallel, even in the darkest pages of the annals of mankind, for anything to compare with the inhumanity, the want of charity, indulged in by the leaders and followers of Communism. Not content with revolting against God, they have indulged in blasphemy, and have exhausted their criminal ingenuity in scourging the best and noblest of men. Such opposition to charity has disgusted the upright of heart.

Though the Jews deliberately subjected Our Lord to this cruel treatment, yet Jesus freely willed all the suffering and humiliations inflicted on Him, and this out of love for us.

THE MEANING OF THE CROWN OF THORNS

Despite all that has been said, a great mystery lies hidden in the crowning with thorns. To us it seems so directly opposed to the dignity and majesty of the Godhead, that it would almost seem impossible that a God should be treated in this way, and rejoice in the humiliation. So opposed is it to the notions of man that we can say for certain that if anyone but Christ had undergone it, his reputation would not have survived. He would have been held in disgrace for ever, and even his friends would have been glad to forget what had taken place. But Our Lord snatched victory from the jaws of defeat, and the crown of thorns has been held in honour by the great ones of the earth. It is really a proof He is God.

It may appear surprising that God should have taken this way to show His love for men. The saints have considered it the refinement of love, but the enemies of God have regarded it as the height of folly. But the saints are right. For what has caused the ruin of mankind? It has been pride: "Pride is the beginning of all evil." (Eccl. x, 15). Christ, in His love, has taught us to despise the glory of this world. Such an *act* leaves an impression that can never be effaced; merely verbal instruction would soon be forgotten.

JESUS ON THE CROSS

Let us now gaze in spirit at Jesus on the cross.

He looks from His bed of pain on the wretches that walk to and fro, wagging their heads, flinging insults at the innocent victim, hurling poisoned darts, that are steeped in the venom of wicked hearts. Yet He does not reproach them, nor does He upbraid the cruel soldiers, who have nailed His hands and feet. No; He prays for His executioners, and does not exclude even the criminal Jews, who have had Him condemned to death. "Father," He says, "forgive them, for they know not what they do." (Luke xxiii, 34). What a contrast is Jesus in this to others who were crucified! The condemned would curse, blaspheme and despair, but Jesus blesses, glorifies His Eternal Father, and succeeds in converting even one of the thieves crucified with Him.

His ears hear the vile curses and dreadful blasphemies of the inhuman mob. His throat is parched with thirst: "My tongue hath cleaved to my jaws." (Ps. xx, 16). His hair clotted with blood falls in a tangled mass upon His shoulders.

THOSE FOR WHOM CHRIST DIED

We must, if we are to form a correct idea of Our Lord's infinite love for men, consider the guilt of those for whom Christ died. He died for all, for the millions, who have been or will be on this earth till the end of time. St. Paul, in several of his Epistles, paints a vivid picture of the times in which he lived, and such lurid shadows could be matched by almost any period of the world's history. Such a spectacle of depraved humanity was not of such a nature as to entice the devotion of anyone to their cause. For when Christ died all peoples, with the exception of some in Palestine, were sunk in idolatry, in atheism, in crimes crying to heaven for vengeance, in an immorality that was extremely loathsome. Even among the Jews, some were not without guilt: some had lost the faith, others blasphemed, most were prepared to sacrifice their eternal to their temporal interests. In truth, the nation, which had once been so dear to God, was now expending its energies on contemptible trifles. And as for the rest of the world it had for thousands of years been descending into a sink of vice.

Men and women adored sticks and stones as gods, deified the most abominable passions, and considered worthy of adoration monsters who wallowed in prostitution, drunkenness and lying. Everywhere Satan reigned supreme, so that he could truthfully say, when tempting Our Lord, that the whole world was his. Truth itself seemed to have disappeared, in great part at least from the earth, for only sparks of it appeared from time to time among the philosophers.

And though such people were most degraded, they considered

themselves the cream of perfection. Their hearts were in the wrong place, and they were determined to keep them there. Such a spectacle is so degrading as to make honest men blush with shame.

And what shall we say of the paganism of to-day? Who would be so bold as to allege that the people, who live to-day, are not as wicked as those who lived in ancient times? It has been said that Judas would be a gentleman compared with some of the enemies of Christ to-day, and that Herod would scarcely be a hypocrite, if placed by the side of those who judge not the wicked, but the just in our times. But enough. Well, indeed, is it that Christ died for the world, otherwise it would be much worse than it is.

Surely this is the acme of perfect love. Christ in agony for the most depraved, the most cruel of mankind.

HIS HANDS AND FEET ARE NAILED

It is difficult to make ordinary people realise the bitter sufferings Jesus endured when His hands and feet were nailed to the cross. It is probable that the wrists of Christ were nailed[1] as, if the palms had been nailed, there would have been the difficulty of their supporting the weight of the body, whereas in the wrists there is a bone that can withstand such a strain. The nails in the feet were driven through the bone that is strong enough to support the entire body. These nails, however, did not break any bones, for they found their way through a body, of which the Holy Ghost had said: "You shall not break a bone of Him." (Exod. xii, 46, Num. ix, 12, John xix, 36). On these nails Christ, as a divine Victim, was hanging for three hours, and owing to the weariness experienced, a languor,

---

[1] If the nails had been driven through the bones in the hands near the wrists this would be quite in harmony with St. John's Gospel, xx, 27: "Put in thy finger hither and see my hands."

which was very agonising, was caused. This increased as the weary hours of the agony wore on.

St. Bridget of Sweden has described in vivid and beautiful language the appearance Jesus presented as He was hanging on the cross: "He was now breathless, exhausted and in His last agony; His eyes were sunk, half-closed and lifeless: His lips were hanging, and His mouth open. His cheeks were hollow and drawn in, His face elongated and His countenance sad; His head had fallen on His breast, His hair was black with blood, His stomach collapsed, His arms and legs stiff and His whole body covered with wounds and blood."[1]

In this as in all revelations we have to consider how much is coloured by the person's own mental outlook. St. Bridget's Revelations, however, have received the special recognition of the Holy See, which has declared they are very edifying to read. This does not mean that all in them is perfectly true to life. Still we can rest assured they are substantially correct.

In these wounds the Saints have always delighted to dwell, drawing from them all necessary aid. As the world is so sensual, its allurements needed the medicine of the Crucifixion to counteract their poison.

But it is no exaggeration to state that the wounds of Jesus are the privilege of sinners rather than of Saints.

THE BODY OF JESUS EXTENDED ON THE CROSS

The cross to which our Saviour was nailed was so fashioned, whether by accident or design, that the places arranged beforehand, to which His hands and feet were to be nailed, did not exactly correspond with Our Lord's body. The result was that His body had to be extended on the cross. Very probably this

[1] Revel. Book i, c. 10, and Book iv, c. 70.

was done intentionally by His enemies; because they had already beheld so many heroic examples of the fortitude of Jesus, and there is scarcely anything more calculated to stir up cruelty in the hearts of men than a display of eminent virtue in him they are persecuting. In this matter it is amazing how far those who have allowed themselves to be prejudiced by hatred will proceed. When the arms of Christ were stretched, the bones in the Saviour's breast were dislocated, and we are not surprised to find Our Lord make known to one of His servants that of all the pains endured in His Sacred Passion, this was the most severe. This was a hidden suffering, known only to Jesus Himself and His Eternal Father, and perhaps in a general way to those who caused it. And why did Our Lord allow this to take place, as He could have escaped it, had He so wished?

To make reparation for the criminal excesses of the human heart. How little it takes to cause one of the smouldering fires of pride, anger, ambition, jealousy, or revenge, to burst into devastating flames! And when they do, men seem to forget all the mortification they have already practised. We see this especially in worldly people who exercise authority. When they consider they are thwarted, or their authority scouted, they resent it bitterly, and often permit a torrent of rage to sweep over them, that drives them to acts of injustice. It is impossible to reckon the havoc such an outburst causes not only in their own souls, but also in those of others, only to be followed perhaps by a fit of remorse, that drives them to the verge of despair.

OTHER SUFFERINGS

There were many other sufferings in the body of Our Lord in addition to what has been mentioned. Occasionally there would sweep over Him an agonising attack, which would bathe His body in perspiration. But I realise as I write that it is better not to develop further the intense bodily sufferings of Our Lord, as some people are so constituted that the mere reading of such outrages overwhelms them even to prostration. We must leave it to the lovers of contemplation to discover what, in addition to those already mentioned, were the sufferings the Son of Man endured in His body on the cross. We shall now turn to consider His soul.

THE SOUL OF JESUS

It is difficult for people, immersed as we are in the turmoil of the world, to grasp the interior anguish Jesus underwent on the cross. He Himself quoting the 21st Psalm, said: "My God, my God, why hast Thou forsaken me?" (xxi, 1). Those who have passed through great interior desolation, to which we shall refer at some length in a future chapter, can draw on their own experience to form a picture of this darkness. Not that Jesus, as Calvin blasphemously asserted, was in despair; no, it is quite clear from this Psalm that Jesus considered Himself the elect of God. On the contrary never was He dearer and more affectionately united to His Father, if indeed this were possible, than at this time; for never did He make such heroic acts of love. In fact, it was impossible for Our Lord to despair; for He always enjoyed, even when on the cross, the Beatific Vision, and this taking away all possibility of His having the virtues of faith and hope, removed likewise all possibility of His losing them. But, by a special dispensation, He permitted that the interior consolation, which ordinarily accompanies the Beatific Vision, be withdrawn during His agony.

There is a mystery in this interior anguish. True He understood as no one but Himself could, how many, in spite of all His sufferings, would deliberately plunge themselves into hell. He could have exclaimed with the Psalmist: "What profit is there in my blood?" This undoubtedly caused much of the desolation.

Yet even on the cross Our Lord, in spite of all, experienced a sense of joy. He knew His Sacred Passion was most pleasing to His Father, and making atonement to the outraged justice of the infinite God would be celebrated in Paradise throughout endless ages. Before His eyes passed the long line of those who would be ardent lovers of the Crucified, and some of whom would, like St. Paul, preach the Crucifixion in season and out of season, while others would never grow weary of contemplating that emaciated body, and that desolate soul in agony. Those in the bitterness of desolation would unite their sufferings to His, and drink even to the dregs the chalice of which He was drinking. Besides, the very nature of heroic virtue, as we have already said, enables one to embrace the most difficult works, even death itself, with delight. But someone may object: If Jesus had delight would this not render Him a less perfect Victim? No: He is made the more perfect Victim because of this spiritual joy: "In every gift show a cheerful countenance, and sanctify thy tithes with joy." (Eccl. xxxv, 11). And St. Paul says: "God loves a cheerful giver." (11 Cor. ix, 7). Besides, He allowed, even on the cross, the Good Thief to participate in this joy, as also the Church, when He constituted Mary its Mother.

Moreover, the Sacrifice of Calvary was the climax of creation. To this had all men, through the promise of a Redeemer, looked forward with wholehearted confidence for thousands of years, and to it the world would, for thousands of years, look back. What a victory, then, was this! And as no one understood this better than Our Lord, no one could rejoice in it better than He.

SORROWFUL LOVE

If anything could move the heart to sorrowful love it is reflecting on the sufferings of Christ. These, like darts of fire, pierce the heart, and cause the will in a spirit of sorrow to grieve for its sins. "*Its sins,*" Yes, because the human will alone is the deliberate cause of sin. The stronger our love grows the more intense becomes the hatred of sin. And this commences the purgation, which will continue as long as the faults are present, striking even at the roots, and destroying them by persistent attacks. To do this the more effectively we should examine our consciences carefully, and take care to remove our predominant passion.

This sorrowful love will induce us to practise penance both interior and exterior.

THE MOTIVE OF THE PASSION IS UNIVERSAL

So universal can this motive be that it sometimes colours all the acts of one's life, thoughts, words and deeds. It can commence the spiritual life in purgation, but it can also continue it by inspiring us in the illuminative way, and perfect it by uniting us to God. It also fosters recollection, which is the secret of conformity with God's will.

CHAPTER V

Divine Love and Sanctity

THE LOVE of God is Sanctity.

This is evident from the teaching of Our Lord. He taught that God is perfect, and He who is perfect is holy, nay, God is infinite in sanctity. Any other sanctity is but a ray of light and heat shot forth from Him. Consequently union with God, which renders us like Him, makes us holy. But union with God is effected by divine love. "He who is joined to the Lord," says St. Paul, "is one spirit." (1, Cor. vi, 19). And it is charity or love that unites us with God. (John xiv, 23).

Our Divine Saviour, being asked on one occasion what was the great commandment explained it in the following terms. "Thou shalt love the Lord thy God with thy whole heart and with thy whole soul, and with thy whole mind and with thy whole strength. And the second is like to it; Thou shalt love thy neighbour as thyself. There is no other Commandment greater than these." (Mark xii, 30, 31). The greatest means the most important. What renders a command most important? Three things: (1) Its power, when observed to obtain for us most surely the end for which we have been created. Charity does this. We have been created for God, to enjoy the Beatific Vision, and charity, with which grace is always associated, assuredly brings us to God; (2) Its giving life, merit and energy to these qualities, which are rewarded when we obtain our end; (3) Its giving us a foretaste of eternal life, nay, an introduction to the life we are to lead in eternal bliss. Charity effects this.

St. Thomas, with his customary accuracy, explains the nature of the obligation each one is under to love God. But before quoting his words, we must premise that these are to be understood reasonably. They mean to love God with all our powers, yet that such love, and such acts of love be compatible with human nature, especially if it, as frequently happens to-day, be a little deranged. Such acts must be in harmony with the duties of our state in life, and with that tranquillity that should accompany us throughout life. While we love Him, making thoughts, desires, words and deeds expressions of the love in our hearts we are not so to rivet our minds on the consideration of God, as to cause a severe strain and lead to the neglect of our affairs. To keep our minds always directly attentive to the divine Presence would require a special grace such as was given the Blessed Virgin, and some of the Saints. No; a general intention of doing all to please God, making acts when we can do so fervently and sweetly, having God as our final end, is quite enough. We shall have more to say on this point when discussing recollection.

The following is the explanation of Our Lord's words, as given by the Angelic Doctor.[1] "We are obliged to direct our whole attention to God, which is the meaning of the words: 'With thy whole heart' and to submit our intellect or understanding to God, which is signified by the expression 'With thy whole mind' and to obey God in every act, which is denoted by: 'With thy whole strength.' "

We are to love God then with all the affection and strength of our wills; we are to think on, pray to and contemplate Him, and we are to submit our passions and senses to the dictates of God's will, and these we are to do, not in a half-hearted manner, but with all our strength.

St. Alphonsus[2], quoting St. Francis de Sales, has admirably

[1] Sum. Theol. ii, ii, Q. 45, A. 5.
[2] Practice of Loving Jesus Christ i, 1.

asserted: "Some place their perfection in austerity of life, others in prayer, or in frequenting the sacraments, others in bestowing alms, but they are deceived, for perfection consists in loving God with our whole hearts." Now, neither of these Doctors wishes to cast contempt on mortification, prayer, the frequenting of the sacraments or the giving of alms, for all these are recommended by Christ, but they wish them used as means to acquire perfection.

The objection is easily made, I have heard it frequently: "This is very good, but is it not somewhat nebulous? We should prefer something more in the region of practice, and less in that of theory."

But the love of God is most practical, as one can see by recalling the various practices, easy and difficult, already pointed out, of loving God.

DIVINE LOVE KEEPS US UNSPOTTED FROM THE WORLD

Those who love God find little difficulty in carrying out the injunction of St. James: "Religion clean and undefiled before God and the Father is this: to visit the fatherless and widows in their tribulation, and to keep oneself unspotted from the world." (i, 13).

The world strives unceasingly to make us its slaves. But by the world we must not be understood as referring to everything in the world, for many things on earth are necessary, and when used in moderation keep us unspotted. It is rather the evil spirit of the world which leads to the abuse of God's gifts, and to withdrawal from His service. There are some who profess to follow only such a worldly spirit. They take satisfaction in promoting their worldly interests, and are ever eager to win the young and influential to their side. In this they act with consummate cunning, and frequently succeed in sowing poisonous weeds in the hearts of the unwary. To gain their ends they take pains to convince their victims that they act entirely in their interests as friends. This is surely contemptible. Would it not be more manly to be straightforward, more honourable to refrain from corrupting the simple of heart? But then this would not gain their ends; for though straightforwardness, like honesty, is the best policy, it is not always the most lucrative.

But let the young and innocent be courageous. They have their lives before them, which they can either make or mar. By upright action, by following the excellent principles of the Catholic Church, they may bring on themselves the ill-will of the wicked. But let them not forget they are on the right side, that they who laugh last laugh best, and that the possession of a good conscience is a treasure to be appreciated.

Two then seek for your heart; the world and Christ. The world has nothing to offer you but a tawdry show, poisonous pleasures, dangerous company, and the tortures of the damned; but Christ calls you to give Him your heart and He will give you peace and happiness. St. Augustine assures us of this: "Thou hast made us for Thyself, and our hearts are restless till they rest in Thee."[1]

SELF-ESTEEM

This evil spirit of the world engenders a self-satisfaction, which is properly termed vanity. Vanity, a daughter of pride, and the very soul of self-love, attacks the glory of God, and wrestles from Him the honour that accompanies our good works. We know that our supernatural works cannot be performed without the aid of grace, but our corrupt nature, craving for the admiration of praise, refuses to recognise this truth, and very gladly opposes it.

This self-satisfaction engenders pride, and causes the loss of

[1] Confessions i, 1.

grace, and with the tyranny of the first, and the absence of the second, sinful habits reassert themselves. Sometimes God, to humble such self-esteem, permits the wayward one to fall into a grievous and most humiliating sin. And yet the remedy is ever at hand. When we realise we are drifting into this vanity we should turn immediately to the practice of humility, have recourse to prayer, and firmly resolve to escape from the meshes of such self-love.

HOW THE LOVE OF GOD SANCTIFIES

Having dealt with the two great obstacles to the growth of divine love in the human heart—worldliness and self-esteem— we turn now to a more congenial subject, and inquire how the love of God *directly* sanctifies the soul. It does so, needless to say, gently and softly, like the rain of a summer's day, falling on the parched ground and reviving every blade of grass, every flower and fruit. In the first place, it introduces the Three Persons of the Adorable Trinity into the soul: "If anyone love Me, he will keep My word, and My Father will love him, and We will come to him, and make Our abode in him." (John xiv, 23). And where the First and Second Person of the Holy Trinity are, there must also be the Third; for all Three have the same essence or nature: "The charity of God is poured forth in our hearts by the Holy Ghost who is given us." (Rom. v, 5). This union with the Blessed Trinity is a real one, by which God resides in the soul as in His own temple. This union becomes very sweet and delightful; for we love the Father, the source of the Blessed Trinity, and realise that it is His Power which has created all things. He is ever old, yet ever young, and the close relationship into which we are brought with Him, and which causes us to know Him more clearly and love Him more ardently, is due to our Redemption by Jesus Christ. We love the Divine Son, the Substantial Image of the Father, as Spouse of our souls, because only by union with Him can we lay claim to the Beatific Vision. We love the Holy Ghost, the spirit of truth, by whose infinite mercy we are advanced in charity and sanctified. "The Holy Ghost being sent down from heaven, on whom the angels desire to look." (I Pet. i, 12). In this we have a pure love that illuminates and transforms.

Let us see what St. Thomas[1] says of this deeper knowledge, and more ardent love of the Holy Trinity: "Above and beyond the common mode, there is a special one belonging to the rational nature, by which God is said to be present as the object known in him that knows, and as the beloved in him that loves . . . According to this special mode, God is said not only to exist in the rational creature, but to dwell there as in His own temple." The more perfect the knowledge and love, the more perfect is the union. This, however, is rendered more thorough by the three gifts of the Holy Ghost: understanding, knowledge and wisdom.

WHAT IS A GIFT OF THE HOLY GHOST?[2]

A gift is a supernatural habit bestowed on the soul with sanctifying grace, to enable the intellect of man to receive divine inspirations. Such a gift, as being something that is purely spiritual, is grasped by faith, and can be understood as existing in the soul by its effects. These inspirations come like a flash, pointing out the right way. They enable souls to practise extraordinary or heroic virtue, and to persevere in grace till death. They are in harmony with the teaching of the Church, and directions of superiors; they bring peace, inspire humble

[1] Part i, Q. xliii, A. 3 (of Summe Theol.).

[2] These pages on some of the gifts of the Holy Ghost are not intended to be a treatise on the subject. Such properly belongs to a work on the virtues of Christ. Only those gifts dealing directly with charity are here treated. Readers wishing to pursue the subject further will find a popular explanation in "The Seven Gifts," by B. J. Kelly, C.S.Sp. (Sheed and Ward, (1941)).

sentiments of ourselves, and assist us to practise prudently a high degree of virtue. But should the inspirations received be opposed to such principles, they should be rejected as suspect, as proceeding either from our own imaginations, or the suggestions of an evil spirit. We should pray to make good use of these inspirations, so that they may impel us to the practice of virtue.

We shall now treat of understanding, knowledge and wisdom.

(A) UNDERSTANDING

Knowledge of God is derived from considering deeply the truths of *faith*, which have been revealed by God Himself. By the gift of understanding, we are enabled by the illuminations of the Holy Spirit—for the lights He bestows come, as a rule, through the gifts—to have a better grasp of, and deeper insight into sublime mysteries. As the eagle, soaring into the heavens, can gaze on the sun, so the intellect of man, illumed by the gift of understanding, can gaze on the divine mysteries, admire them, understand and be influenced by their hidden meaning. It is by the wonderful light, given by the gift of understanding, we can contemplate not only the Passion of Jesus Christ, but the mystery of the Blessed Sacrament, the adorable Trinity, the angels and Saints. This light is necessary if we are to attain fully the end for which we have been created. By it we come to realise, as we never did before, the unity of the Godhead, the mercy of the Incarnation, the value of the Precious Blood, the marvellous results of sanctifying grace, the infinite glory of the Beatific Vision, the perfecting of the soul, wrought by prayer and the seven sacraments, and the singular privilege of the Immaculate Conception of the Blessed Virgin. St. Paul, writing to the Ephesians (1, 18) refers, in the following terms, to the gift of understanding: "I cease not to pray to God to grant you that you have the eyes of your heart enlightened, that you may know what is the hope of your calling, and what are the riches of the glory of his inheritance in the saints."

(B) THE GIFT OF KNOWLEDGE

This gift bestows on the mind of man the power to judge correctly, enlightening him to know what he ought to hold by faith, and pass a correct judgment on things.

But what is the difference between knowledge and understanding? Some consider it lies in this, that the gift of understanding renders the mind fit to grasp the truths proposed by faith, and penetrate into their very heart, while the gift of knowledge is concerned with practical matters. But this is not the opinion of St. Thomas, for he says:

"If we consider the matter carefully, the gift of understanding is concerned not only with speculative,[1] but also with practical matters, as stated above (A.3), and likewise the gift of knowledge regards both matters, as we shall see further on (Q. ix, A.3), and so we must distinguish in some other way. For all these gifts (wisdom, understanding, counsel and knowledge) are ordained to supernatural knowledge, which in us takes its foundation from faith. Now, *'faith cometh by hearing'* (Rom. x, 17). Hence some things must be proposed for the belief of man, not as seen, but as heard; to these he assents by faith. Faith, first and chiefly, is about the First Truth,[1] and in the next place, about certain considerations concerning creatures, and furthermore extends to the direction of human actions, in so far as it works through charity, as appears from what has already been said on Q. iv, A.2, ad 3.

"Hence, on the part of things proposed to faith for belief, two things are needed on our part. First, that they be penetrated or grasped by the intellect, and this belongs to the gift of

[1] "Speculative matters" mean the theory, apart from practice, about things·
[1] The First Truth is God, Who is Truth Itself.

understanding. Secondly, it is necessary that man judge these things aright, that he judge he ought to adhere to them, and withdraw from their opposites; and this judgment, with regard to things divine, belongs to the gift of knowledge."[2]

We find this gift marvellously exemplified in the lives of all the Saints. St. Teresa, St. Francis de Sales, St. Alphonsus, could discourse on the most sublime truths, with a sound judgment, yet immediately afterwards prove themselves quite capable of dealing in a practical manner with ordinary things. By it St. Teresa tore the veil from false contemplation, or rather from the extraordinary ways of such contemplation, and unmasked deception; by it St. Francis de Sales practised a wonderful meekness of heart; by it St. Alphonsus, while aiming at the heights of perfection, would descend to sympathise with sinners, and accommodate his directions to the circumstances of their lives.

This gift enables men to unify their spiritual life, combining all its roots and branches in one central thought, which will guide them safely through the maze of sin and error in the world. It enables them to distinguish the natural from the supernatural, the true from the false. It teaches them God's designs, instructing them to look beneath the surface of things, and judge matters at their true value.

(c) WISDOM

"Wisdom is more active than all active things, and reacheth everywhere by reason of her purity . . .

"For God loveth none but him that dwelleth with wisdom.

"For she is more beautiful than the sun, and above all the order of the stars, being compared with the light she is found before it.

"For after this cometh night, but no evil can overcome wisdom." (Wisd. vii, 24, 28-30).

[2] Sum. Theol. ii, ii, Q.8, A.6.

Of all the gifts of the Holy Ghost, wisdom is the greatest, because it judges of things in the light of the First Truth, and sets in order all things according to divine rules. While it casts a flood of light on revealed truth it is, however, subject to faith. It is the result of charity, yet perfects charity.

Wisdom is subject to faith; for though no evil can come near wisdom, yet we learn of wisdom through experience,[1] i.e., by the sweetness that accompanies it. The light is there, but, in the beginning, it is not so easily perceived as the sweetness that makes the impression. In fact, we often find ourselves make acts of love to God, and when we seek the cause discover that wisdom has been active. After some time we can trace the sweetness to the thought—the Divine Goodness, the Passion, the Blessed Sacrament, etc., from which it arose. Now, were one always sure the sweetness were the effect of wisdom, and that wisdom was making known the truths that impress us, there would be no danger of deception. But this is not so. For sometimes the imagination can deceive us, and even an evil spirit can assume the form of an angel of light. When there is question of faith, there is no danger of being led astray. Its truths have been revealed; they are proposed to us by the infallible authority of the Catholic Church, and therefore when followed they remove all danger.

A person is said to be wise in his knowledge of a science when he has mastered its root-idea, can deduce its principles, and apply them to concrete cases as they occur. This is precisely a question of judging according to the master-idea.

In a similar way a man is wise in the spiritual life when he has in his intellect the gift of the Holy Ghost, termed wisdom, by which he can, through his sympathy with divine things, form a right judgment about them. He sees things, if we may use a bold figure, through the eyes of God. "The spiritual

[1] Of course we learn of it also by faith (Isaias xi, 23).

man," says St. Paul (1 Cor. ii, 15) "judgeth all things, and he himself is judged of no man." This gift enables the mind to grasp clearly that God is the Creator of all things, Supreme Ruler of the world, upholder of all that exists, whose will nothing escapes, and that all occurring in the world, sufferings, persecutions, trials of the just, temptations of various kinds— all come from His hands, and tend to His glory. If one, endowed with divine wisdom, considers the life of Christ, he beholds where the world sees folly, only supreme wisdom, and grasps, if he is to attain his end, the necessity of becoming one with Him by charity. But how does wisdom perfect love? By divinizing charity, by purifying and perfecting all the virtues, enabling us to perform their acts with marvellous perfection. It casts a practical light on the mind, and lets it learn by experience that God is a tender Father, a spiritual Bridegroom.[1] Such thoughts show us how sweet the Lord is, and cause us to relish His divine presence. They forge a bond between God and the soul, that is as strong as death, and this strengthens divine love in the soul. When the human will resigns itself into the divine hands it experiences a flood of delight. This reacts in outbursts of love. It then produces acts of adoration, praise and joy, with great ease. The will now desires to advance to that union which God has designed for it. But since man cannot in this life reach the fruition of such desires, he wishes to be dissolved and to be with Christ (Phil. i, 20). He even looks forward to death with joy, subject however to the divine will; for while a desire to be united with God in Paradise is virtuous, a desire to die and escape the sufferings of this life would not be; but to desire to pass from time to eternity and there contemplate and enjoy the Beatific Vision, would be. In this way, the soul advances from one degree of love to another, and reaches sanctity.

[1] These words, though metaphorical, were used by Our Lord in Matt. xii, 50, etc.

LOVE PERSONIFIED

The soul enamoured of God turns with delight to the place where He dwells on earth, the Tabernacle, where Christ is to be found. Our Lord revealed to one of His servants that He had instituted this sacrament of love, especially for those devoted to Him, so that He might keep them company in this vale of tears, and preserve them to labour in His interests, and so embellish their crowns.

The Holy Eucharist is the throne of love. Here Jesus, the fairest of the children of men, lies hidden under the white vesture of the Sacred Host. Nothing appears here but the inventions of love. His Divinity is hidden; for its majesty would terrify our weak human nature: His Sacred Humanity is concealed, lest its perfections keep us at a distance from Him. And here the infinite God, whom the heaven of heavens cannot contain, multiplies Himself, wherever a priest and altar are to be found.

St. Thomas, quoted by the Council of Trent, teaches that the object Christ had in view when bestowing us the Eucharist, was to increase charity in our hearts. In the Eucharist we have the Victim of love, Love Personified.

Love is self-sacrifice; now, the Mass is a sacrifice to God and for man, a never-ending sacrifice, that will continue till the end of time. Love is the communication of oneself, the outpouring of the heart on the object loved, and this God has so done in the Eucharist as to arouse the admiration of the angels themselves. It is the greatest favour He could bestow; it is an infinite gift; love is the lowering of oneself, the placing of oneself on an equality with the one loved, and Jesus has done this in a way that no imagination, however vivid, could anticipate. It raises the loved one up, and clothes him, if we may say so, with the transforming robe of God's love. Love takes delight in being loved, in being united, by a union of will, to the one loved, and in making the loved one like the lover himself. The Eucharist, while uniting us to Christ, causes us to bear a strong resemblance to Him. In fine, true love finds happiness with the object loved, and where could there be greater happiness than in union with the Holy Eucharist?

LOVE IS THEREFORE SANCTITY

From what has been said, it is evident that divine love is sanctity. Saint Thomas holds that sanctity consists in purity, firmness, and a union in the soul of all the virtues (ii, ii, Q. 81, A.8). Now love of God unites all these; it renders us pure, for by it we are united to God, Who is purity itself; it renders us steadfast, urging us to strive always till after death we reach more fully the Object loved: "Put ye on the Lord Jesus Christ, and make not provision for the flesh in its concupiscences" (Rom. xiii, 14). St. Francis de Sales says that when the virtues are perfect in the soul, there is never one without the others. But they are rendered perfect when charity has become perfect in the soul. In this then we have absolute sanctity.

AN OBJECTION

Some may allege: Is not the love of God in danger of developing into self-love, emotionalism, softness? Certainly not. For love of God is shown by deeds, and should a man allow himself to swerve from the path of virtue he will soon find his love of God grow cold; for graces are withdrawn, the heart grows hard, spiritual death ensues.

IT IS THE SAFE WAY

To point out the sure and safe way to holiness and eternal bliss, I will quote here from the Instruction by Monsignor Alfred

---

[1] St. Francis de Sales: Love of God, Book xi, C.8.

Ottaviano, at the time Assessor of the Holy Office, and which was published in *Osservatore Romano*, 4th February, 1951. It emphasises what has been said in this chapter, while warning us against dangers that allure by their attractive appearance.

"For some years," said the Monsignor, "we have witnessed an increase of popular hankering after the wonderful, even when it concerns religion. The faithful repair in vast crowds to places where visions and wonders are supposed to take place, and at the same time abandon the church, the sacraments, preaching and instruction. People, ignorant of the first words of the Creed, set themselves as ardent apostles of religiousness. Some of them hesitate not to speak of the Pope, the Bishops and the Clergy, in terms of severe reprobation, and then grow indignant when the latter do not take part with the mob, in all the enthusiasm and outbursts of popular movements . . .

"A good Catholic knows that in the saints themselves the nature of sanctity consists not in the supernatural gifts of visions, prophecies and wonders, but in the *heroic practice of virtue*. That God should in some way authenticate holiness by miracles is one thing, but that holiness consists in performing miracles is another. We must not confound holiness with what can be, and as a rule is, an unmistakable sign of holiness, but not always sufficiently clear as not to need the necessary supervision of ecclesiastical authorities."

For all of good will such words will be sufficient to detach them from the extraordinary ways of the spiritual life, and lead them to pray for and practise that love of God which will enable them to acquire a high degree of virtue.

LOVE, AN EXCELLENT SIGN OF PREDESTINATION

Man, when on earth, is sometimes harassed by doubts about his eternal salvation; but the Catholic Church, Christ's repre-

sentative on earth, has given a number of signs to indicate
whether we are or are not on the way to heaven. Some of these
are the following: (1) to live the life of a good Catholic, (2) to
hear and profit by the preaching of God's word, (3) to cultivate
a tender devotion to the Blessed Virgin, but (4) spiritual writers
assert that one of the surest is to possess charity, or the love of
God.

It is the Eternal Father, foreseeing that some would correspond with grace, perform good works, and die in His friendship, Who predestines them to eternal glory. St. Paul has said:
"He chose us in him," i.e., in Christ, "before the foundation of
the world, that we should be holy and unspotted in his sight
in charity." (Eph. i, 4).

We can see from these words that it is divine love, which we
have acquired by the merits of Christ, that decides our lot for
all eternity.

The same St. Paul assures us we shall reach eternal happiness
if we render ourselves like Jesus Christ; "Whom he foreknew,
He also predestinated to be made conformable to the image of
His Son, that He might be made the first born among many
brethren." (Rom. viii, 21). How are we made like Christ? By
the practice of His virtues, especially charity.

We may add it is not a very profitable question to discuss:
Are we predestined or not? What is more important is to do
the works of God by which our justification and election are
assured. For God always renders to every man according to
his works.

CHAPTER VI

Prayer

THIS CHAPTER makes no pretence at giving a full treatment of the subject of prayer; it would require a volume much larger than this to do justice to so wide, and so sublime a subject. No; the object is less ambitious. It is to point out for those who would love God ardently the necessity of prayer, and especially of the prayer of petition. It will aim also at assisting those who do love Him to pray more easily and sweetly.

WHAT IS PRAYER?

St. Augustine states[1] it is a devout conversation with God, the emphasis being laid on the term "devout," which signifies respectful, affectionate and in conformity with the divine will. St. John Damascene[2] says prayer is the raising of the soul to God, i.e., a lifting up of mind and heart from a natural state to a supernatural union with God. It is an act of the virtue of religion. For as by religion we recognize the infinite majesty of God, and the depths of our own nothingness, so by prayer we adore, praise, thank, love and ask Him for favours. In this way we humble ourselves in the divine Presence. It is in reality an act of mind and will addressed to God. We have both *vocal* and *mental* prayer; yet we should fail to pray, were we in parrot-like fashion to repeat only the words.

The Apostles had often seen Our Lord pray; they knew He had spent forty days and nights in prayer, indeed He seemed always to be absorbed in prayer, and they naturally concluded

[1] In Psalm 85 N. 7.
[2] De Fide Cath. Book iii, C. 24.

it was a most important exercise for all who would gain the end for which Christ came on earth. Guided by a special inspiration of the Holy Ghost, they came to Him and said: "Lord teach us to pray." (Luke xi, 1).

And what kind of prayer did He teach them? He gave them the "Our Father," in which He struck the note of simplicity, the true note of all genuine prayer. It is this that in a special way renders our prayers pleasing to the Most High.

VOCAL PRAYER

Jesus began by teaching them vocal prayer, because He wished to teach a form of prayer suited to every capacity, and adapted to all times. In the "Our Father" we have an universal prayer, one that the poorest intelligence can grasp, one sufficient to satisfy all needs, and yet one of which the greatest genius could not sound the depths. And let us not forget that Jesus was here instructing Apostles, men who were called to preach His doctrine throughout the world, destined to reach marvellous heights of sanctity,[1] seal their faith with their blood, and ultimately become great Saints in heaven.

EXPLANATION OF THE "OUR FATHER"

In this prayer we have an introduction, and seven petitions. By it we ask God for all the necessities of soul and body.

In it Our Divine Saviour instructs us to call God, Our Father, reminding us that by the state of grace, we are made the adopted children of God, brothers of the Divine Son, and brothers of one another. By these words we recall His majesty and glory, and render Him reverence, fear and love.

Then follow three petitions, addressed to God, each of which contains an act of perfect love to Him. We pray that He may be praised, adored and glorified by His creatures, that the

---

[1] All except one—The Iscariot.

thrones in heaven, vacated by the fallen angels, may soon be filled, and that the divine will may be accomplished as perfectly on earth as it is in heaven. To these three blessings, which resound to the divine glory, there is added another, requesting a favour for ourselves. We ask Him to give us to-day the food we need. In this petition there is also a reference to the Holy Eucharist.

We then request to be delivered from three evils: (1) from our sins, (2) from temptations into which we should fall were God to withdraw His saving grace, (3) from temporal evils.

Though the "Our Father" is short and simple, yet by it we can acquire a high degree of sanctity. St. Teresa says she knew a woman who, by reciting it slowly and with reflection, succeeded in reaching the state of contemplation.

CHILDLIKE PRAYER

The first prayers we said were short; in them only the names of Jesus and Mary were repeated. In course of time, however, we advanced, and recited the "Our Father" and "Hail Mary." We were told to keep our minds fixed on the prayer, and not to allow them to wander through distractions. Such prayers, ascending from innocent hearts, were surely among the best we ever said. And yet how simple they were!

He who would preserve the childlike spirit of prayer, and render his prayers efficacious, should pray with humility, for would it not appear unseemly in a beggar to seek for alms with a haughty air? And what are we in the sight of the God, to Whom we pray, but beggars? However, even though we are mendicants, yet being His children we should pray with confidence in the divine goodness. This simple trust wins the Heart of God, and brings us many blessings. We should pray also with resignation to the divine will, leaving our petitions in His hands, since He knows what is most to our advantage, and lastly we should pray with perseverance.

But why is prayer necessary?

Because, in our struggle against our inclinations and the powers of darkness, it is our great weapon of defence. Our inborn weakness, when there is question of practising virtue, and conquering temptations, is astonishing. Often the passions rebel against God and reason, and we need special grace to repel their assaults. God has promised to give these graces to those who ask for them, and generally they are granted to those alone. Consequently in time of serious temptation, and such comes occasionally in the lives of all, we shall not conquer unless we pray, and continue to pray all the time we are tempted.

In addition to this, or rather because of this, we are expressly commanded by God to pray. The Scriptures are teeming with examples that illustrate the necessity of fulfilling such commands. St. Luke says that Our Lord "spoke a parable to show that we ought always to pray and not to faint." (xviii, 1). And the same Evangelist states that Jesus said to His Apostles in the Garden: "Pray lest ye enter into temptation." (xxii, 40). In several of his Epistles St. Paul insists on the necessity of such prayer: "Be constant in prayer." (Col. iv, 2). "Pray at all times in the spirit." (Eph. vi, 17, 18); "Pray without ceasing." (1 Thess. v, 17).

PRAYER OF THE HEART

The soul that truly loves God is not content with addressing Him merely with vocal prayer; for as it is the heart and not the lips that love God, so it is the heart that ardently desires to speak to Him. In fact, nothing gives greater joy to such a person than to spend a quarter of an hour in presence of the Blessed Sacrament, and there hold a heart to heart conversation with God, hidden in the Eucharist. He approaches Him humbly, knowing well that humility is the best introduction to the Presence of the infinite Majesty of God. Then he begins to pour forth his secrets into the Sacred Heart. He recounts his troubles, anxieties and necessities, the sufferings endured, the humiliations received, the opposition borne—all of which are but items in his daily routine, and he gazes in wonder at the crucifix standing above the Tabernacle, and realises, as he never did before, how trifling are his annoyances, compared with the sufferings Christ endured on the cross. And then grown calmer, he exclaims: "O my God, I have not yet resisted unto blood, and you have shed the last drop of your Precious Blood for me." And then, forgetting self and thinking only of God, he continues: "O Lord, I believe Thou are present in the Blessed Sacrament. What a sacrifice Thou hast made to give us this inestimable gift! No other than Thy death on Calvary, for the Mass, by which we receive the Holy Eucharist, is the sacrifice of Calvary." Who but God could have wrought so many miracles to leave us Himself in this Sacrament? Truly this act of love is infinite. And how many virtues does the Sacred Host recall to our minds! Its whiteness reminds us of purity, its roundness of eternity, and the fact that at the voice of the priest He descends on our altars, of obedience.

At other times, but especially at Pentecost, the fervent will think of the Holy Ghost, Who is love itself, descending on the Apostles in the form of tongues of fire, and the wonderful mission He has, since that time, carried out in all parts of the world. This fire reminds the soul of love and having reached that point the soul remains there, for St. Mary Magdalen de Pazzi has wisely stated that we can proceed no further than love.

It should be stated, however, that in souls that are seraphic, and many whose causes for canonisation have been introduced seem to have been of that class, the love in the will far exceeds the light in the mind; for as a little spark can kindle a great conflagration, so a little ray of truth can cause an all-consuming fire of love. Is this not making the effect greater than the cause? No; for this extraordinary flame is due to the direct action of the Holy Spirit. It is here the gift of *piety* comes into operation; for the soul understanding by the light received that God is a most tender and affectionate Father, approaches Him with unbounded confidence, gratitude and delight. This, however, in no way lessens the reverential fear a child has for its parent; for such fear leads to treating God with the respect He deserves.

O my God, the love, burning in the heart of the Saints, transformed them into the fire of perfect charity, and this implanted in their souls all virtues in a high degree. Has not St. Ambrose said that "Piety is the foundation of all virtues?" In this way the soul becomes one with God.

PRAYER IS THE REFLEX OF OUR LOVE

When I wish to know what I look like, what I am, I glance at my image in the mirror. In a similar way, if I wish to learn how I love God, I have but to turn to the mirror of prayer, especially prayer of the heart, and there I learn the exact proportions of my charity, whether it is little or great. I know it is very little indeed, if when an opportunity for praying occurs, especially if my needs demand it, I turn aside from prayer and seek distraction in worldly trifles. It is well, however, to remember that to fulfil social duties, to make calls that etiquette demands, especially when these are carried out in a spirit of charity, must not be classed as trifles. These are really virtuous acts. It is rather the desire to indulge in dissipation, that destroys the spirit of prayer. I must not be surprised to find if I withdraw myself from God, He will withdraw Himself from me. Again, should I find prayer full of aridity and rather difficult to make, and then gladly seek the opportunity of avoiding it, I am made conscious of my deficiency in self-sacrifice. Or if I go to prayer to enjoy consolation, not to strengthen myself for the conflicts that lie before me, I have reason to fear I am guilty of what St. John of the Cross terms the fault of "spiritual gluttony" and must, by mortification, use for the glory of God the sweetness that heaven bestows. Or, if when deluged with consolations, I grow vain, and fail to give God the glory that is His due, I am guilty of "spiritual pride," one of the most poisonous weeds I could foster in the garden of the soul.

But if on coming to pray I find myself drawn to union with God, and can speak to Him with my whole heart, or rather am glad to let Him speak and pray within me, I have excellent grounds for concluding that in my ordinary round of duties I have not been dissipated, but genuinely recollected. Above all, if when I am privileged to receive consolation I am pleased to obtain a favour that comes from the generous Heart of God, and if He were to withdraw it, and plunge me into desolation, I should be equally pleased, then I can rest assured that I have made some advance in the love of God. For I realise that in both instances I am fulfilling the divine will, and, because I have no special choice, I am attached not to the consolations of God, but to the God of consolations, and so am treading the straight road to a nobler and a better life.

HOW PRAYER OF THE HEART IS MADE

The desire the loving soul experiences of being one with God can be satisfied only by devoting itself from time to time to considering Him, and the truths He has revealed. To do this the more easily I would suggest that the reader set aside half an hour, or at least a quarter of an hour daily to think only of God, and His mysteries, and to make acts of love to Him. For this purpose it would be well, especially in the beginning, to read a spiritual book, so that these truths may sink deeply into the mind, make an impression on it, and enkindle in the

heart the fire of love. We need not be at pains to make many
acts, nor need there be much speaking, for Our Lord has warned
us to avoid this when we pray, (Matt. vi, 7), nor need we be
anxious to ask many favours: "for your Father knoweth what
is needful for you, before you ask Him." (Matt. vi, 8). Anxiety
would disturb the mind, and render calm and peaceful prayer
impossible, whereas resignation of ourselves into God's hands
and the making an effort to follow the divine light will cause
our prayer to be well made.

I am here confronted with a serious problem and feel I should
betray cowardice were I not to answer it. It is this. Many
people dread the name of mental prayer, imagining it is something rather difficult and mysterious, capable of being grappled
with only by the stalwart minds and hearts of priests and religious. Such a notion is very far from the truth. In fact, many
Catholics, almost without being conscious of it, make mental
prayer frequently. Each time they listen attentively to a sermon,
and reflect seriously on the subject treated, making at the same
time an application of the matter to their own conduct, forming
acts of sorrow, of love and of purpose of amendment, they have
made mental prayer and have made it well. Or if they read a
spiritual book, hold conversation with a spiritually-minded
person, or make the way of the cross, eliciting the acts we have
indicated, they have really made a meditation that would satisfy
the wishes of St. Alphonsus.

At the same time, I must confess there is some little *difficulty*
occasionally in making meditation. There is aridity of which
there will be a full treatment in a later chapter. Still such aridity
need not deter us; a trifle such as this should not turn us from
the love of God. A little fortitude—and *fortitude* is one of the
gifts of the Holy Ghost—will work wonders. Besides, aridity,
generally speaking, is but a passing phase, by which no one
need be deterred.

On the whole, prayer is *not* difficult. The one who loves God looks forward to it gladly, goes to it eagerly, endeavours to make it well. With it life is made sweet and easy; without it life would be intolerable. We are told that the Saints and servants of God used to go to meditation, visit the Blessed Sacrament, and make such exercises, as a famished soldier, engaged in forced and laborious marches, would go to a well-set table, where he would find much to appease his hunger. And these remarks apply more to mental than vocal prayer.

LET US ENDEAVOUR TO MEDITATE DAILY

We shall now consider why we should devote some time daily to mental prayer.

In the first place meditation, i.e., considering revealed truth, loving God, and resolving to serve Him better, will, if perseveringly pursued, introduce us into a new life, will throw light on the mysteries of faith, will add a charm to, and clothe in a robe of glory, the most common, the most uninteresting labours of our daily experience. But if we do not meditate, we shall believe in the truths of faith; but we shall fail to realise them, fail to appreciate them, fail to draw from them all the strength and manliness and love we should, fail in fine to make them the guiding stars, the living realities of our lives. We shall never, without meditation, be privileged to grasp something of the infinite immensity of the Almighty, the marvellous union of the three Persons of the Blessed Trinity, Who are bound by a knowledge, love, and infinite perfection surpassing all the created mind can conceive. We shall never realise the infinite act of love there is in the Incarnation of Jesus Christ, unless we meditate on this mystery. We shall never know how much God loved men, unless we think upon, thank and love Him, for redeeming us by the birth, the life and death of His Divine Son. Again, if we fail to meditate we shall never come as close to God as we desire. We shall never be embraced by that intimate touch of the Almighty, which raises us above self, above the things of time, gives us a foretaste of eternal happiness, and opens up vistas of the eternal, and insinuations of the great things that are to come.

Meditation contributes to strengthen our love of God. It makes an impression on us that remains for life, and becomes the motor-power of our actions. When the priest preaches, the light and fire acquired by meditation will manifest themselves in his sermons and instructions, and will bring untold blessings on his labours. Otherwise much of his work will fail to hit the mark. Why? Because the grace, the unction, the power, which are so essential to succeed in dealing with souls, are wanting. And if he doubts this, let him plunge his heart each day into the furnace of divine love, enkindled by meditation, and he will draw it forth, inflamed with zeal for the glory of God, and then let him compare the results of his ministry in each case.

In the next place, sin, even serious sin, may remain steadfast in the soul, refusing to be dislodged, even though vocal prayers be said daily. For the occasions of sin still remain strong, bad companions are not avoided, even sensual pleasures are not sacrificed, because the things of earth have entered too deeply into the soul, and have ousted the things of the spirit. But this cannot happen if we daily make meditation. Grace will enter so deeply into the soul, devotion to God will so affect the heart, that no peace, no happiness will be experienced till the offending monsters have been cast forth.

Again the extraordinary graces we need to advance and climb the heights of divine love will be denied us, if we do not meditate. For this reason St. Alphonsus assures us it is morally impossible for a religious to be a good religious, who does not make meditation. Priests, by reason of their state, are required to lead virtuous lives; as their lives are spent in treating with what is most holy. Good meditations make saintly priests. And as for the laity, their spiritual lives will fail to develop, their love of God will, as a rule, be rather weak and unproductive, unless they make an attempt to meditate. At the same time they need not have any elaborate system, though it is well to use one in the beginning. After some time meditation will develop into affective prayer, and then the system may be discarded.

In the last place all will conquer temptations more easily, will refuse to make peace with their faults, will make a success of life, and will welcome death more calmly and sweetly, who are faithful in making meditation well.

Realising then the precious blessings that meditation brings, the soul devoted to God will gladly embrace the opportunity of being drawn into closer union with Him by mental prayer.

AVOID DANGERS

Experience teaches us there is nothing so sacred but the perversity of man can contaminate, nothing so secure but the inconstancy of man can overthrow. And so it is with prayer. Although it is a very safe way to reach heaven, and is a necessary means to advance in divine love, yet it can be, and has been seriously abused. Those of an emotional temperament, with a longing for the admiration of others, have sometimes fallen victims to vanity, and instead of using prayer to advance them in humility have used it to inflate their minds with pride. Others, having an itching for extraordinary and dangerous ways, have gone after the butterflies of fancy, and abandoned the path of solid doctrine. They have become dupes of the evil spirit, and have in the end lost every particle of grace. Against such dangers we would warn the fervent, and insist once more that the safe way in prayer is by humility, resignation and obedience.

On the other hand God has raised elect souls in His Church to edify and instruct His people, and with them has made use of extraordinary means. There have been such extraordinary saints as St. Joan of Arc, St. Gerard Majella, St. Margaret Mary, St. Gemma Galgani, etc., who, led by extraordinary ways, reached heroic sanctity. They had an extraordinary mission to fulfil, and succeeded marvellously. They were visibly protected by God, yet when called by God to abandon the beaten track, they passionately besought Him to lead them by a less dangerous path, i.e., by an ordinary way, and it was only when they were certain that if they resisted, they would run counter to the divine will, that they gladly followed the way God was leading, and achieved the end in view. But in all this God watched over them very carefully, protected them from others and themselves, shielded them from the attacks of the worldly. But God has by no means promised to do that for those who rashly depart from the ordinary way, and who are more anxious to acquire a reputation for sanctity, than sanctity itself. Nay, we might say that such people would run a risk of being rejected by God.

MEN AND WOMEN OF PRAYER

The Saints, who have been given us as models to imitate, were men and women of prayer. It was the atmosphere in which they moved, the very air they breathed, the power-house that kept the love of God at the height of fervour, the strength that enabled them to practise sublime virtue, the ever-ready means given them by God to obtain grace, perseverance and the crown. When darkness cast a shadow on their souls, when persecution and failure dogged their footsteps, when friends had dropped off, and new enemies had arisen, it was prayer that enlightened, consoled and fortified them. It was a general means, that suited all, and which, therefore, was easy, and it was a sure means, because once the few and simple conditions needed to render its efficacy infallible, were fulfilled, it brought the all-powerful remedy.

With it the poor become rich, without it the rich are poor; with it the shackles of sin are cast aside and the ornaments that adorn the soul, as the bride of Christ, are assumed; with it death and hell are vanquished, and man's way to Paradise enjoys a foretaste of the eternal years; without it sin, misery and all the evils that accompany eternal death fall on man.

In every state of life we find souls who enjoy a wonderful gift of prayer. Sometimes amid the most unfavourable surroundings, there springs up a lily of exquisite fragrance, a rose of marvellous beauty, endowed from on high with the dew of heavenly prayer. They receive the favour with thanksgiving, they preserve it with humility and charity. We read in the life of St. Aloysius that he would spend a very long time in prayer, yet would never suffer the least distraction. In the case of St. Catherine de Ricci, it was noticed that even as a novice she was always rapt in prayer, and this spirit she preserved all her life. It was said of the Venerable Father Passerat, an early Redemptorist, who spent all the time, in which his duties did not engage him, in prayer, that he fulfilled perfectly the advice of Our Lord: "Pray always." (1, Thess. v, 17; Luke xviii, 1). But of such souls we should say not so much that they always prayed, but that the Holy Ghost prayed always within them.

Among the Apostles, St. Paul enjoyed the gift of prayer in a sublime degree, though indeed all the apostles were distinguished in this respect. Yet somehow from the Epistles of the Apostle of the Gentiles we learn more of his spirit of prayer than from any other works. What a flood of light inundated his mind! What flames of charity consumed his heart! We note too, if we read carefully, that he never separated the life of action from that of prayer. Each assisted the other. By his fervour in prayer he laboured zealously for the glory of God, by his zeal in the practice of virtue he prayed with the greater fervour.

We shall discuss the question of prayer no further here, even though some readers may consider the treatment of so important a subject rather *jejune*, reserving for Chapter VIII, that on "Life," an explanation of affective prayer, and the prayer of simplicity, as also the question of contemplation, which some regard as one of the divisions of prayer. Still these questions must not be considered as dealt with exhaustively, but only in so far as they affect divine love.

CHAPTER VII

Recollection or Walking before God

WHEN ST. THOMAS AQUINAS was studying at Naples, he would often attend the Dominican Church there, and was so attracted to the way of life the Fathers followed that he asked and obtained their religious habit. His family, learning of what had taken place, grew indignant, and determined at all costs to withdraw him from the influence of the Dominicans; but the Fathers hearing this sent him to Rome, from which he was to proceed to Paris. After leaving Rome, he was attacked by two of his own brothers, who were in the service of the Emperor. They made him a prisoner and brought him to Rocca Secca, their ancestral home. Here they threw him into prison. He was subjected to very harsh treatment; but he, keeping before his mind the words addressed by God to Abraham: "Walk before me and be perfect." (Gen. xvii, 1), ever walked in God's Presence, doing all to please his Divine Master; and so remained steadfast in his vocation. The brothers, however, hoping to weaken his resolution, concocted a plan to make him commit a sin against chastity, thinking that if they succeeded in this they would cause him to grow disheartened, and abandon religious life altogether. For the purpose of temptation they introduced into his room a woman of evil character; but St. Thomas, realising what her designs were, seized a burning faggot from the fire, intending to strike her. She, seeing what he was about to do, screamed and ran in terror from the room. Then the Saint, tracing with the burning brand the figure of a cross on the wall, knelt to thank God for delivering him from so pernicious an evil, and besought Him to grant him the gift of perpetual chastity. This favour the Lord was pleased to grant, so that the Saint was never troubled by temptations contrary to chastity again.

This incident is here related to prove that if we walk before God, and think of Him, we shall surely be protected from the snares of our enemies.

To act in this way is sweet and easy; for the heart that loves God—and where is the heart that would be so ungrateful as not to do so?—finds in Him the object of its affections, and turns to Him with the same vigorous tendency as the magnet does to the pole. And once the soul has contracted this habit, it turns to Him again and again, and on each occasion experiences a new sensation of delight. It never tires of One, Whose conversation is without bitterness, Whose presence without tedium, Whose gifts without repentance. His store of riches is infinite; from it He draws the most precious treasures to enrich them that love Him. "With me are riches . . . that I may enrich them that love me." (Prov. viii, 18 and 21).

The enamoured soul is not obliged to traverse the seas to discover the One Who gives joy to its heart. He is found everywhere: "for in Him we live, move and are." (Acts of Apost. xvii, 28). He is found above all in the soul of the just; "If any one love Me, he will keep My word," says Our Lord, "and My Father will love him, and We will come to him, and make Our abode in him." (John xiv, 23). This Infinite Good is an endless ocean of Being, from Whom we cannot escape. He is in the air we breathe, in the water we drink, in the beautiful sights we behold; He is in everything, not, indeed, in a pantheistic way; but He is there by His power, because He sustains and preserves all things; He is there by His essence, because being infinite, He fills all space.

This exercise was a favourite with the saints, and should

make a special appeal to all who would love God; for in reality it is a continual act of divine love.

Before describing the fruits, produced by recollection, I must show from three great authorities, modern and popular, that recollection pertains to charity, and that, without it, a work on charity would be very deficient.

"It is an infallible rule," says St. Alphonsus, "that love is increased by the presence of the object loved. This happens even among men, although the more they converse together the more their defects are discovered. How much more will the love of a soul for God increase, if she keeps Him before her eyes; for the more she converses with Him, the better she understands His divine beauty and lovableness." (Vera Sposa, c. xvi, 8, 3, n. 7).

Fr. Mouton, C.SS.R., commenting on these words of the most Zealous Doctor, says: "Recollection is the offspring of charity, and in its turn both nourishes and strengthens love of God, which, without it, would soon grow cold, just as a piece of iron does, when removed from the furnace that supplies its heat. But if it remain united to God, the soul will feel itself more and more inflamed with love for the Infinite Beauty." (Monthly Virtues: Vol. III, p. 199).

St. Teresa frequently states in her writings: "A true lover always remembers the beloved." This is the very nature of its love; for to think of God, converse with Him, express its amorous affection—these are the substance of its life.

The author of the life of St. Francis de Sales assures us he always had the same even temperament, was always meek, affable and lovable, and always had about him that peace that was derived from union with God. These were the result of his recollection.

Recollection then is so closely connected with divine love that without it charity would languish, and grow cold.

EXCELLENT FRUITS DERIVED FROM
THIS PRACTICE

As motives urging us to put into practice the exercise of God's presence, we shall state some of its chief blessings.

In the first place, it is very effective in assisting us to conquer assaults of passion, especially if these be violent. These onslaughts, it is true, are made only at intervals, but as we do not know when such attacks may take place, we must be always on our guard, that they may not take us by surprise, and overthrow our virtue. Of one thing, however, we can be certain, that when we come into contact with an object that excites them, they become more violent in the contest they wage. Sometimes, like savage wolves, enraged with hunger, eyes flashing fire, fangs exposed and saliva dripping from their jaws, they leap fiercely at their victims. Above all, if they have already acquired the habit of having such revolts against the All-holy satisfied, what power can keep them under restraint? Nothing but the grace of God, which is given liberally to those who ask it. But people who live habitually in the divine Presence, and have acquired a sensitiveness of conscience, will, on feeling the hot breath from these monsters, immediately fly to the God of their hearts for protection.

We all know how well a soldier fights in presence of his General, especially if he be a man whom he loves, and whose friendship he cherishes. There is no cowardice betrayed; no turning the back on the enemy. Or take another instance, that of a business man explaining the value of his wares in presence of one who can forward his interests. He takes care to manifest his gift of influencing others, and uses all his persuasion to lead the customer to make a purchase. Well, God's eyes are ever on us; He knows how we act; where His interests are at stake, if we act carefully, wisely and zealously, we shall receive a great reward.

Seneca, writing from Rome to a friend, who had gone to one of the Roman Provinces to assume a position of importance, advised him, if he wished to succeed, to act always as if the eyes of one, for whom he had great respect, were ever upon him. Now, faith teaches us we are ever in God's presence, and if we sin, we offend the divine justice, whereas if we act nobly that same justice, which is nothing else than divine mercy, will treat us benignly.

During a war, which took place in the present century, a soldier, while fighting in defence of his country, was very severely wounded. In his illness he was visited by his Prince, who treated him with marked kindness, expressed deep sympathy for his sufferings, and showed his appreciation of all that had been endured. The young man was deeply affected by these attentions, and ever afterwards spoke of the affair as something worthy of remembrance. And yet in expressing his compassion for a fellow-man, this Prince only expressed a feeling which was but a ray of the infinite compassion of God for us. How much more eager should we be to receive the approval of God on our actions than this soldier was to receive the approbation of an earthly potentate!

The most excellent of all fruits that come from the cultivation of the divine Presence is one to which we have just referred, namely, that God sees all the acts of our lives, and for these, if well done, grants an eternal reward. Such a thought will urge us to do always what is pleasing to God. Our Lord, speaking to the Jews, said of His Eternal Father: "I do always the things that please Him." (John viii, 29). In this most of us are deficient; for we fail to do *always* what pleases Him. Some when at prayer are recollected, but cast it aside when prayer is over, and so neglect to do their duties well; others at meals please God by the mortifications they practise, but fail to mortify their eyes, ears and tongues at other times, and others again are delighted to remain with Christ on Mount Thabor, and partake there of supernatural joys, but do not relish the tedious and painful hours on Calvary. The faithful soul will as a rule be asked to spend but a comparatively short time on the mount of suffering; for God, knowing our weakness, does not try us beyond what each can bear. But the exercise of God's presence will enable us to accept calmly the sweet and the bitter, knowing that both, being expressions of the divine will, cause Him much pleasure, when well received. At one time, perhaps, it is our faith that is tried, but encouraged by the divine Presence we despise the tempter, and come forth triumphant, or at another we may be tempted to lose confidence, but on appealing to God we regain our unwavering trust. Or our minds perhaps are inclined to neglect penance, pass over what we know is the more pleasing to God, and choose the easier way. Vanity, impatience, immodesty may urge us to self-indulgence, but in all these we conquer, because we remember God, Who died for us on the cross. We then experience that delicious sweetness that springs from the habits of tried virtue. Of course those who are favoured with the gift of infused recollection will be able to put all these, that have been suggested, into practice with great ease, and much interior joy, for they will hold an almost continuous conversation with the God, Whose Presence they experience within them. In this way, the truly recollected give all for All. They make a genuine offering, and there is no rapine in the holocaust. This is most acceptable to the Most High.

THE THOUGHT OF GOD'S PRESENCE INCREASES DIVINE LOVE

We know that friends who are absent from each other for a long time, and who fail to correspond, will, in spite of the close friendship they had once cultivated, be ultimately forgotten. But should a mere token be exchanged it will suffice to preserve affection warm in the heart; for it will cause joy to spring up afresh. But even though one friend does visit another, yet should he, during his visit, perceive that the other continues to be absorbed in trifles, refuses to speak, and even acts in a discourteous manner, will this unseemly conduct not destroy friendship altogether? Certainly it will. Now God, our Best Friend, visits us, abides within us, unceasingly bestows marks of His friendship on us, and how worthy of contempt and indignation would be our attitude were we to refuse to recognise His Presence within us, neglect to thank Him for His favours, refuse to entertain Him as a friend should be entertained!

Most of us desire to put into practice the injunction of Our Lord to pray always. This, of course, does not mean that we be ever moving our lips, but it means, as we have said, that we turn occasionally with tender affection to Him, express our wish to be ever constant in His service, unite our wills with His, and request Him to grant us the favours we ask.

LIGHT IN THE MIND

But if we are to practise this satisfactorily we must take care to carry it out sweetly and calmly, without forcing ourselves to adopt systems, with which neither our aptitude, nor the circumstances in which we are placed, agree. This we shall do if we take care to correspond with the graces and inspirations we daily receive from the Holy Ghost.

There are many ways in which the mind can accustom itself to remember the Divine Presence; but among this number are two, which I specially recommend, and which I shall now proceed to explain.

The first consists in remembering that God, being infinite, is everywhere, sees our most secret thoughts and actions, approves of what is good and chastises what is evil. Reason arguing from nature to nature's God, can reach this conclusion, and faith, which gives us greater certitude than reason, contains it among its revealed truths: "In Him we live, move and are." (Acts xvii, 28). This is an excellent method which, without any strain, or any images formed by the imagination, can be easily practised. Indeed, all things being created by God, can remind us of their Creator.

To realise this we shall now consider in the light of faith some things that have come into existence only within recent times, and shall see how they remind us of God. This is all the more necessary, since we live in a material and sensual age, in which men and women, eager to avoid the difficulties and partake of the luxuries of life, forget their God, and forget all about the eternity to which they are hastening. Unlike the pagans of old, we might say that those of the modern world do not try to deify their passions, rather they try to deify themselves. This is all the more amazing since the misery and corruption of men, so far from making them gods, has not made them good angels, not even good Christians, but has sunk them in the depths of depravity. Communism has to a large extent given an impetus to this debauchery, and though upright men and women abhor the abominations that turn them from the path of rectitude, yet insensibly the sensuality of this age weakens their desire to practise virtue. The gratification of self has now been reduced to such a fine art that the good old remedy for the ills of man, mortification, has practically been banished from the face of the earth. Some indeed, who are devoted to the service of God, still practise it, but they are few. What is the result? The world is invaded by scorpions, that sting the bodies of men, causing them intolerable pain. Nature is taking a dread revenge on those who violate her laws. And yet, throughout it all, God rules the world, bringing good out of evil, permitting souls to descend into crime, so that they may in disgust turn away from it, or if they will not, that the spectacle of such corruption may turn the upright away from the course the wicked are pursuing. The world to-day, as it did before the birth of Christ, groans for a deliverer, yet a deliverer shall not be given it, but the Christ, Who by His Passion and Death, has already redeemed it.

But how can we by means of what we see and hear practise the presence of God? We can ascend by easy steps from nature to nature's God. In the spring we hear the birds, pouring forth their flood of song, and thrilling the world with their music. Later the leaves come out on the trees, the flowers spring up, and a healthy glow beams on the earth; the beauty and perfection of which remind us of the infinitely perfect One, Who has made them, and bestowed on them the splendour they enjoy. Then, in the warm days of summer, all things grow and increase around us, reminding us to grow daily in the virtues of Jesus Christ, especially in that of charity. Then autumn, when the fruits fall plentifully to the ground, brings to our minds the liberality of Him, Whose goodness has bestowed such an abundance of what is desirable. Winter, when the leaves have fallen from the trees, and frost has spread itself over the earth, reminds us of death, through the portals of which both the good and bad have to pass to receive their retribution, be it good or evil.

But let us address ourselves to what daily confronts us.

Lo! there is an *aeroplane*, whizzing over our heads, and making such a noise as to arrest our attention. The machine is the result of man's ingenuity, and puts us in mind of the divine intelligence, to which the brightest light of the human mind is but a faint ray in the midst of much darkness. This is a gift from God and man for which we should be grateful, for it has rescued many from corporal and spiritual danger. It reminds us too that men who have laboured so strenuously to attain this triumph in time, should strive as courageously to win a victory in eternity. Or perhaps we gaze on a *steamship*, that gracefully glides through the waves, carrying its passengers, amid a variety of comforts to a distant land. It reminds us we too are quickly passing over the waters of life, and making for the shore of the world to come, and if we can ill bear with the discomforts of this life, we shall find it much more difficult to bear with those of the next. Or we are reviewing the means of travelling at our disposal to-day; trains, buses, motor cars, etc. Truly luxury is the boast of our modern civilisation; but it demands a heavy toll in the weakness and sickness of the human race as it is to-day. Or we go to the cinema for an evening's entertainment; but is it always entertaining, at all events in a way that does not leave a nasty wound on the conscience? Or we turn on the *wireless*, which often gives us useful lectures, broadcasts on scientific and other subjects by those who have specialised in such branches; but sometimes too there is an immoral play, or a scene from the lowest walks of life that reflects little credit on the producers. What a world of good both it and *television* would achieve, were they run on lines that would be an honour to God and man!

Sometimes we are forced to witness a rather humorous spectacle—for we have it on reliable authority in the daily press —of a man, who having outstripped his fellows by a few votes, considers himself another Napoleon and infallible in his pronouncements, awaits but an opportunity of launching an attack on the Church. But do not such people, contrary to their designs, only serve to write across the pages the heroic virtues of the ecclesiastics they persecute?

It may be that from what we read we learn and are shocked at the immorality of the world. Yet we must be edified at the patience of God, Who does not interfere with man's free will, but invites him to repent, and do penance for his sins.

Some are heard to say: "The Catholic Church, when her

influence is compared with what she exercised in other centuries, occupies a mediocre position among the great ones of the earth to-day." Does she indeed? She is the *only* power that thrives more on the frowns than the smiles of potentates. For 300 years she dwelt in the Catacombs, and seems to have felt more at home there, than when achieving victories in the palaces of kings.

LOVE IN THE WILL

The exercise of the Divine Presence, commencing in the light of the mind, is completed in the love of the will.

St. Francis de Sales and St. Alphonsus were quick to grasp that the fervour of a meditation, well-made in the morning, will soon evaporate, unless some fuel be added to keep the fire alive. What they recommended to their followers was to exercise themselves in making frequent and fervent ejaculations. These, like darts of fire, would spring from the heart, pierce the Heart of God, and bring down a shower of graces on souls.

Unless, however, we accustom ourselves to practise solitude of heart, creatures will make such a noise in us that we shall seldom be inclined to speak to God at all. For if we allow ourselves to be unduly distracted, at one time by the pleasures, at another by the cares of the world, we shall be anxious to converse with and about them. The Servants of God were convinced of the necessity of being at times alone with God, if they were to enjoy that freedom of God's children, which is the balm to heal all sores, the medicine to cure the evils of the heart. St. Catherine of Siena, being compelled to pass much of her time in the midst of her family, where the drudgery distracted her, complained of this sweetly to Our Lord, and was instructed to make a solitude in her heart, where she might at any time retire to hold conversation with her Divine Master. Once she had grasped, and put into practice, this excellent method, she never again experienced the slightest difficulty in preserving recollection.

Even though we make ejaculations, we shall find it useful to turn to God at stated times during the day, and address ourselves fervently to Him. We can do this when we wake in the morning, and retire to rest at night; for as the Lord is the beginning and end of our existence, it is but just that we commence and end the day with prayer. If we are able to attend Mass, and receive Holy Communion daily this will be a very meritorious way of commencing the day, and will make it comparatively easy to turn to God at any time. I say "comparatively easy," because sometimes, without any apparent cause, we feel a disinclination to rise above the natural level. When this occurs we should practise patience, profess our weakness and inability to effect anything supernatural without the aid of divine grace. We shall also find it very suitable to make at times a visit to the Blessed Sacrament, and say the Rosary of the Blessed Virgin.

SPIRITUAL READING

Another excellent means of keeping oneself recollected is to read for some time each day a spiritual book. Each one, of a pious disposition, has some special devotion, e.g., the Blessed Sacrament, the Sacred Passion, Our Blessed Lady, to which his heart is attached; why not read the life of a Saint who cultivated such a devotion! St. Alphonsus, St. Gerard, indeed all the Saints were fervent lovers of Jesus and Mary, and we shall learn from their lives how they practised devotion to them. In this way we shall fill our minds with elevating thoughts, which will make a special appeal, and keep us in union with God and His Blessed Mother.

I should add, however, that the way to cultivate recollection is not to multiply devotions, but to endeavour sweetly and calmly to keep ever in the Presence of God, and do all things to please Him.

THE THREE KINDS OF SOULS

At various times we experience distinct inclinations towards certain practices of virtue, and these give us an indication of what kind our souls really are. Souls may be divided into three classes, corresponding to the different ways in which they practise prayer and charity. These are angelic, cherubic and seraphic. *Angelic* souls labour with much constancy, are careful of the smallest details and succeed by their efficiency. To such a class belonged unquestionably St. John Berchmans, who, little given to emotion, made every act of his life an act of virtue. Next, there are *cherubic* souls, such as St. Thomas Aquinas, St. Ignatius, St. Teresa and St. Francis de Sales, who received floods of light from the spirit of divine Truth, and explained with marvellous lucidity very intricate problems. They threw much light on the higher states of prayer, the love of God and the mysteries of our religion. Such people fill an important position in the Church, and carry out successfully the difficult missions entrusted to them. Lastly, there are *seraphic* souls, who burning with a most ardent love of God, desire to do great things for His glory, and the salvation of their neighbour. They aim at doing always what is as pleasing as possible to the Most High. They meet with severe crosses, their prayers are not always saturated with the honey of consolation for very often they have to endure aridity. By these their loyalty to God is tested. Among these may be reckoned Saints Bernard, Francis of Assisi, Bonaventure, Clare, Margaret Mary, etc. It is not easy to decide exactly to which class a particular Saint may belong. St. Alphonsus seems to have enjoyed in an eminent degree the qualities that distinguish all these classes. He was most painstaking in his work; cast, as Doctor of the Church, a flood of light on many difficult questions, and was certainly inflamed with a most ardent zeal for the glory of God, and the salvation of souls. Still, in the life of each Saint, one class generally predominates, and this points out of what kind that Saint really is.

DESIRES

If we wish to advance and persevere in this spirit of recollection, we must cultivate ardent desires to acquire holiness, which is nothing else than perfect charity. Such desires direct the aim of the archer, sharpen his arrows, and cause them to stick fast in the target at which they are directed. And should this archer be fighting a battle for his life against the enemies of his soul, these desires will strengthen him to ward off the attacks and strike a crushing blow at the foe that is endeavouring to destroy him. Then in the hours of peace, when he is seldom hard-pressed, and is inclined to grow weary of well-doing, these desires renew his valour and urge him to aim higher. Men scarcely ever do anything great or even important in the spiritual life unless they cultivate ardent desires; but if they do nourish them, they will find that when they are fervent, they are nearly always efficacious. "To the just, their desires shall be given." (Prov. x, 24).

Our Lord encourages such ardent desires. At His Last Supper He said: "With desire have I desired to eat this pasch with you before I suffer." (Luke xxii, 15). i.e., I have most ardently desired it. What peace do ardent desires, when realised, bring the heart. "The desire that is accomplished delighteth the soul." (Prov. xiii, 19). The Epistles of St. Paul, the reflection of Christ's teaching, are replete with expressions of His fervent desires.

Still, our desires must be more than mere desires; they should enable us to realise what we have at heart; for the Scriptures say: "Desires kill the slothful, for his hands have refused to work at all." (Prov. xxi, 25). Those who take no care to translate their desires into acts, grow lazy and achieve nothing; but the true lovers of God are not lazy, they see so much in the wilderness of the world calling to be reclaimed, that while their lives last they must make strenuous efforts to bring about the desired reform.

CHAPTER VIII

Life

THIS BOOK would be very inadequate in its treatment of charity did it fail to treat of life in its relation to the virtue that gives supernatural life to the soul—charity.

What then is life? Or to put the question in a more concrete form, when do we say a thing lives? When by reason of its own nature it can move itself. For instance, we say a man lives because he can move himself by walking or running; in other words he has power to reduce a part or parts of himself from potentiality to act. This does not mean that all in him is in act, but it means that while he lives there is one faculty at least, the will, that is in act. On the other hand, we do not say a machine lives, rather we say it is without life, because it requires to be moved by something exterior to itself, for example by the hand of man, which either turns a handle, or, by means of an electric switch, sets the machine in motion.

On this earth we have three different kinds of life. The vegetative, life in its lowest form, the sentient as in animals, and the intellectual life in its highest form, as in man. Man is a rational animal. He can feel, suffer, and be in good temper—these he has in common with animals, but he is also rational, for unlike vegetables and animals of the field, his soul can never die. Above him is the angelic life, pure spirits with intellects and wills, but above all is the divine life, or the life of God, in which all is perfection, in which all is in act. God is the original source of all life, having created it. Angels acquire knowledge by intuition; their nature demands it be infused into them by

God. Their knowledge is much more perfect than that in man, for the latter, ordinarily speaking, depends on his senses for the knowledge he acquires. Sometimes, however, God is pleased, in the case of a few individuals, to infuse knowledge into their minds.

Man, therefore, stands in life midway between animals and angels, higher than the former, lower than the latter. Yet man can, in a marvellous way, climb the ladder of perfection, and become, by sanctifying grace, a partaker of the divine nature, putting on the Lord Jesus Christ, and attaining to uniformity with God's will. This may, in the life to come, cause him to surpass in merits and glory many of the angels. He may be placed, as was said of St. Teresa among the Seraphim, in the highest order of these blessed spirits.

I have already stated that man has a rational soul, and the Council of Vienna has declared that this is the *substantial form* of the body. It is the *form* because it determines the species to which it belongs, and it is *substantial*, because it is a spiritual substance, which gives reality, existence, essence to man. The soul gives life to the body. When the soul departs, the body dies and becomes corrupt.

THE LIFE OF THE SOUL

In the soul we can distinguish two different kinds of life: the natural and supernatural. The natural life and destiny are such as would belong to man, had he been created for a purely natural end, in which, as in Limbo, he would enjoy merely natural happiness.

But as we are treating here of life in connection with charity it is with supernatural life we deal.

Previously we quoted Richard of St. Victor to show there are two ways to develop and perfect the supernatural life, that of Martha and that of Mary. The first is the active supernatural life, the second the contemplative.

THE ACTIVE LIFE

St. Thomas teaches that the active life of the soul consists in the practice of the virtues of Our Lord. But he quotes St. Isidore[1] to warn us that "in the active life all vices must in the first place be extirpated by the practice of good works." But how are vices extirpated? By penance, mortification, and the practice of the other moral virtues; for by these their opposites are removed.

All our duties, with which the moral virtues are concerned, are regulated by the four cardinal virtues: prudence, justice, fortitude and temperance, to which are annexed those virtues that constitute them cardinal. But for most people the six key-virtues embrace their obligations; these are charity, chastity, humility, obedience, mortification and perseverance.

Our Blessed Lord, speaking to St. Martha in her home at Bethany, gave her to understand, as we previously said, that her life of activity was less esteemed by Him than that of St. Mary Magdalen, because the contemplation of the latter would continue for ever. Still, the virtues Martha acquired and practised, though there would be no objects on which they could be exercised in eternity, would nevertheless remain in an eminent state in the life to come, and would merit an immense reward. St. Gregory says: "Great are the merits of the active life, but greater still are those of the contemplative."[2]

As St. Thomas explains this point admirably, it may be well to quote him here.[3]

"The root of merit is charity and as charity consists in the

[1] De Summo Bono iii, 15.
[2] Morals vi.
[3] Sum. Theol. ii, ii, Q. 182, A. 2.

love of God and our neighbour, the love of God by itself is more meritorious than the love of our neighbour. Hence that which pertains more directly to the love of God is generically[1] more meritorious than that which pertains to the love of our neighbour for God's sake. Now the contemplative life pertains directly and immediately to the love of God; for Augustine says (De Civtate Dei, xix, 19) 'that the love of (divine) truth seeks a holy leisure namely the contemplative life, for it is the divine truth above all the contemplative life seeks!' Wherefore the contemplative life is generically of greater merit than the active life. This is moreover asserted by St. Gregory in his Third Homily on Ezechiel: 'The contemplative life surpasses in merit the active life, because the latter labours under the stress of present work, by reason of the necessity of assisting our neighbour, while the former with heartfelt relish has a foretaste of the coming rest.' "

The active life, however, is a preparation for contemplation, for by exercising a high degree of virtue, we prepare ourselves to practise the two together. "Those," says St. Gregory, "who wish to hold the fortress of contemplation, must first of all train in the camp of action."

The active life must sometimes be cultivated, for our very existence may depend on it. It would be absurd for a person to cultivate contemplation, if indeed it was possible, and leave children starving. Daily most of us are called to imitate Our Lord, Who said: "My Father worketh until now, and I work." (John v, 17). Some are so constituted that, if they are to practise contemplation, they must give some time to active work, and others so formed that if they do not work, they spend their time in idleness. Work, moreover, allays the humours of the body, extinguishes the fire of passion, brings peace and con-

---

[1] Generically means as a general rule, though in specific cases, when charity so demands, it is more meritorious to assist our neighbour.

tentment. One who spends a heavy day in working will scarcely ever think of indulging in immorality.

At the same time, if prayer and contemplation do not give vigour to work, the labour will not be well done, i.e., when there is question of supernatural works. For the desire to promote God's glory will not direct it; the eternal reward will not be given. But a life of prayer does direct the aim, enables one to strike boldly, and so gain the crown.

In the Catholic Church there are some Orders whose members devote their lives to active work, and others whose members cultivate the contemplative life. But do not imagine the former give all their time to work, and the latter all their time to contemplation. No; their lives are mixed, though in active Orders the active life predominates, and in contemplative, contemplation prevails.

We read in the life of St. Francis Xavier, the Apostle of the Indies, that he spent many years in active labours for the glory of God, yet during that time advanced so far in contemplation that his active may be considered the result of his contemplative life.

THE CONTEMPLATIVE LIFE

Contemplation is a large word, and I must confess I experienced no little remorse each time I have used it already, without first giving an explanation of its meaning. But I shall endeavour to do so now. The term is derived from two Latin words: "con" "with" and "templum" "a temple." A temple was a place marked out for religious purposes: to honour and worship the divinity. It is not unlikely then that contemplation, which means to consider God attentively and devoutly with the eye of the mind, is so-called because by considering, admiring and loving Him, we become, by sanctifying grace, veritable temples of the Living God.[1]

It may appear to some rather strange that such a word should appear in a popular book. But we must not imagine that ordinary people are unacquainted with it, or better, with the reality itself. While it is quite true that contemplatives are by no means numerous, yet they are met with in nearly every path of life, and not by any means always among the learned. In this matter a little experience conveys more knowledge than years spent in study.

The reader will very probably have noticed that this section is not called contemplative prayer, but rather contemplative life; for it is a state not a passing act. True, he who enjoys contemplation prays in a contemplative way, but this is only one act out of the many he does in a contemplative manner, and such prayer is rather the effect than the cause of contemplation.

That this division of the supernatural life into active and contemplative is an excellent one, we have the authority of St. Thomas, who says:

"Now the intellect is divided into active and contemplative, since the end of intellective knowledge is either the knowledge itself of truth . . . or is some external action . . . Therefore life, too, is adequately divided into active and contemplative."[2]

But in practice what does this mean? St. Gregory tells us: "The contemplative life is to cling *with our whole mind* to the love of God and our neighbour, and to desire nothing beside our Creator."

This simplifies matters very considerably; for it shows that

[1] "Contemplation," says St. Francis de Sales (Love of God C. vi, C.), "is nothing else than a loving, simple and permanent attention of the spirit to divine things." The two essential things are emphasised here: (1) the experimental knowledge of God and (2) Ardent love. These two points are the salient features of St. Thomas' teaching. They make us temples of God.

[2] ii, ii, Q. lxxix. A. 2.

these two ways of life, active and contemplative, aim at attaining the same end—perfect love of God.

THE DEGREES OF ORDINARY PRAYER

We do not get absorbed, and caught up, so to speak, in prayer all at once; no; we advance by degrees, and spiritual writers have very carefully noted and explained the steps by which we proceed.

As has already been stated, when we have meditated for some time, there is, as a general rule, less need for considerations; for spiritual thoughts, especially on the mysteries towards which we have a special devotion, have become deeply impressed on our minds, and are easily recalled when we come to pray. It may be a thought of the Passion, and by reflecting deeply either on the Scourging, the Crowning with Thorns or the Crucifixion, we have grown enamoured of the kindness and love of the Divine Victim, so that when we kneel to pray the thought of Him arises spontaneously, causes us to experience a glow of fervour, and a fire consumes the heart. Or it may be the Eucharist, to Which we are attracted, and the thought of the years Our Lord has remained out of love for us on the Altars, inflames us, and we are led to make affections. With much sweetness we make acts of humility, of love and abandonment to the Divine Master. Or perhaps it is the Divine Infant, that has won the affections of our hearts, and when we behold the Second Person of the Blessed Trinity—infinite in wisdom and all perfection— assume human nature, and embrace out of love for us cold, hunger, thirst and contempt, we are drawn to pour out our hearts to Him in love, admiration, thanksgiving and com- passion. When we experience such sentiments we may rest assured we have already entered on affective prayer, and should not hesitate to cultivate it ardently.

Yet at this point it may be well to sound a note of warning.

When we discover we have, by God's grace, and the aid of the gifts of the Holy Ghost, advanced to affective prayer, we should not, with the eagerness of one who wishes to attain the heights of sanctity over-night, repeat these acts till we strain both mind and heart and act with such violence as to wear out our nervous system. I can quite understand that with some of an ambitious and highly-strung nature the fatigue and exhaustion mentioned by Tanquery[1] may ensue. Lest, however, the fear of such may deter youths from adopting affective prayer, I hasten to add that while I have met very many who made use of affective prayer, I never met even one who suffered from the ailment he describes in No. 985 of his book on the Spiritual Life. But then people of our countries are really matter of fact.[2]

Affective prayer is not acquired suddenly; in fact there is a period in which considerations and affections intermingle, until at length the affections sweetly but surely absorb us all the time.

But you will say: How am I to know for certain, when the change is to take place? The following are the signs that indicate when we should pass from meditation to affective prayer:

(1) When, by dwelling on considerations, we reap little or no advantage from our prayer; for when a thought has struck us, and aroused the affections, which begin to burn brightly, considerations have attained their end, and it would be a mistake to continue to use a means we do not need.

(2) When the mind has quickly and easily recalled some truth or mystery, and has imperceptibly passed to acts of thanksgiving, desire, admiration and love, it would be a mistake to go back and consider, and thus seek to arouse what we already possess.

[1] The Spiritual Life by A. Tanquery SS. Book i, C. i, A. 3.
[2] It may appear to some that this section on affective prayer, etc., would have been more suitably introduced under prayer, in Chapter VII. Still, it was deliberately omitted then to avoid confusing the reader. I should add that as it is a means to acquire sanctity, or the perfect love of God, it can be reasonably introduced at any time in this book.

(3) The soul is now detached from sin, and the heart is habitually united by recollection to the Guest, Who dwells within it. The natural result of this is to entertain this Guest in the way He desires, i.e., by affections, by the love of Him.

ADVANTAGES OF AFFECTIVE PRAYER

The great advantage of this form of prayer is that it increases in a wonderful way divine love in the soul. But, like most gifts that come from God, it carries as a favour some little cross. The strong fervent love, especially if it be of an emotional character, may arouse sensuality, and this instead of increasing may injure divine love. How are we to deal with this attack of the sensitive appetite? We must of course resist it, realising that to consent to it would defeat the end of prayer, play into the hands of the enemy, and rob the soul of the love of God. It would be wise to reveal the difficulty to the director of conscience and adopt the suitable remedies he suggests. Should it, however, persist, we must despise it, and contempt will certainly weaken the assault. To those of good-will God often permits such an attack to withdraw them from the consolations of creatures, attach them to Himself, and lead them to grasp the truth that the love and service of Him are found, not in feeling, but in the determination of the will. When we have mastered this, such attacks will cause suffering rather than pleasure, and we shall be anxious to get rid of them so as not to displease the Divine Master. We might offer ourselves as victims to endure any pain He pleases, rather than sacrifice His friendship, or cause Him the least offence. In this way we shall use the weapon of the enemy to destroy him.

In the next place, this prayer gives great glory to God, for by it we are led to abandon ourselves to God's will. Why is this so? Because the will now reaches a high degree of fervour in practising the love of God, and experience teaches us that the fulfilling God's will is nothing else than the love of God in practice, and to abandon ourselves to the divine will is to fulfil it perfectly. But while we do this, we must take care not to indulge in spiritual pride, by thinking we are saints, and have far outstripped others in holiness. The truth is we are still at the bottom of the ladder and we have many rungs, i.e., degrees in prayer, to climb before we reach the top. Should such a temptation attack us, we should use it to convince ourselves of our weakness and misery, for no sooner has God begun to advance us in the spiritual life, than we take to ourselves all the glory we should give Him. If we wish to go forward one step in the spiritual life, we must take care to avoid pride, which would ruin everything since the sure foundation of all spirituality is humility. Steel your heart against this childish vanity. You must, since it is the worm that eats the heart out of all that is virtuous.

(3) This kind of prayer[1] will bring much consolation, arising from closer union with God, so that we shall, with the author of the Imitation of Christ, exclaim: "To be with Jesus is a sweet paradise." Still, we must remember not to place too much confidence in these feelings, since they are not always reliable, can pass away quickly, and may be succeeded by aridity; for even in affective prayer there can be aridity; yet such aridity, if borne courageously, will produce a very close union with God. Still, feelings of joy are not to be altogether neglected, for such feelings are frequently the result of a more generous outpouring of divine grace, which assists us to do great things for God's glory. When we come to prayer, however, we must not be induced to make it in the hope of receiving such consolations; for this would be to place the consolations of God before the God of consolations; but rather we must come to please God, seek to know His will, and to obtain the grace to practise it.

[1] Can we enjoy the blessing of affective prayer without having had formal meditation? Yes, I think so; for I have met people who prayed *affectively* from morning to night, yet never made a formal meditation.

(4) If we pursue affective prayer with a generous and a humble spirit we shall soon be advanced to the prayer of *simplicity*.

THE PRAYER OF SIMPLICITY

The prayer of simplicity, which we are now about to explain, is admitted by some writers to be of a kind quite different from affective prayer. It is also called the prayer of simple regard, acquired contemplation, etc. Since all admit such a kind of prayer, and explain it in the same way, it would be a mistake to forget the thing itself, and quarrel about terms.

This kind of prayer has always been used by the faithful, though the first reference to it, in any work we have, is by Richard of St. Victor (d. 1172) who explains in what it consists clearly enough, when he says: "The first way (of contemplating) is through human intelligence, the third, by divine grace only, *the middle by the union of both human diligence and divine grace*."[1] But the first to use the term prayer of simplicity was Bossuet (1627-1704) in the directions he gave to the Sisters of the Visitation, who were in his diocese. Among other things, he said:

"The soul by her fidelity to mortification and recollection usually receives a purer and more interior prayer, which we may term the *prayer of simplicity*, and which is nothing else than a simple interior gaze, regard or loving attention, directed towards some divine object, whether God in Himself or one of His perfections; it may be Our Lord Jesus Christ, or one of His mysteries, or some other Christian truth. The soul dispenses with all reasoning, and employs a gentle contemplation, which maintains her in peace."[2]

After his time we find repeated references to this degree of prayer, which by many writers was called "*acquired contempla-*

[1] Benjamin Major (1, 2).
[2] "An Easy Way to Spend the Day in Prayer," N. 3 by Bousuet.

tion." So it is styled by Fr. Paul Segneri, S.J., Benedict XIV, and St. Alphonsus. It is described at some length in Fr. Poulain's work, "The Graces of Interior Prayer." Though the Abbè Saudreau seems to combine the prayer of simplicity with the affective state, Pére Garrigiou-Lagrange, who is the recognised leader of the Thomist School to which the Abbé belongs, states that many theologians accept acquired contemplation. While describing it exactly, he himself prefers to call it the prayer of simplicity. Fr. Gabriel, O.D.C., though he insists more than the others on the infused element in this prayer, accepts the term acquired contemplation, and states it was the Carmelites who chose and explained it first. The term was received, and its limits defined by the Teresian Congress in Madrid, March 1923, at which over 100 Discalced Carmelite Convents were represented, and which was attended also by other religious, notably by the Dominicans. But let us hasten to learn in what it consists.

WHAT IS THE PRAYER OF SIMPLICITY OR ACQUIRED CONTEMPLATION?

It is a kind of prayer which *all* can acquire by means of ordinary grace, the assistance of the gifts of the Holy Ghost, and their own endeavours.

The reader will remember that in affective prayer the considerations are simplified; in the prayer of simplicity they practically disappear altogether. Richard of St. Victor says: "It is a penetrating gaze, which without effort embraces several objects simultaneously." To the ordinary reader these words, if not explained, mean nothing, but when clarified convey much information. We have been accustomed to reflect often on Our Lord's sufferings. Now, when we consider Him in the Garden of the Agony, we grasp by one thought the sufferings He has to endure, the contempt He has to undergo, and then His unalterable patience, meekness and charity, and all come before the mind as by an intuition, so that we grasp several objects at the same time. And this is done with little effort, rather these various aspects occur spontaneously. They make a deep impression; we penetrate their meaning and reach the very heart of the matter. This is what Richard of St. Victor means.

This thought is sometimes presented to the mind in tabloid form, i.e., a text of Scripture comes into the mind, and keeps repeating itself at intervals for some time, such as "Deliver us from evil"; "He was wounded for our iniquities, He was bruised for our sins," and this conveys a mine of information, which we grasp, each time the text repeats itself.

But not only are the considerations simplified; the affections are also simplified. Instead of being numerous, they are now reduced to one, e.g., "My God, I love Thee," or "O God, I am delighted Thou are infinitely happy," or "O Most Blessed Trinity, I adore and love You." And these we can with joy and ease keep repeating for a considerable time. We can see God in everything; the events we hear spoken of we know happen because He wills them; next we come to realise the divine Presence within us, and often during the day hold sweet colloquies with the God of our hearts.

But sweetness and joy do not continue always; there are distractions and aridity in this kind of prayer. We may find it difficult after being saturated with delights to return to the earth and live on "potatoes and salt." This is the best metaphor to explain it; and God expects us to be generous and faithful to Him now in the hour of darkness since it was precisely for this crisis He has bestowed His gifts so abundantly.

It is here the gifts of the Holy Ghost are brought into play; for as this is a prayer of light and love, of thought and affection, we unite ourselves with the life of the Blessed Trinity in making it. This is a life of knowledge and of love, and this is the life we begin really to live. The light of knowledge comes from the virtue of faith, and this faith illumines the mind in a special way by reason of the gifts of understanding and knowledge. In this there is nothing extraordinary, it is the normal development of sanctifying grace in the soul, and there is no one but can acquire it. But this light inflames the will with love, so that charity increases in the soul, and begins to assume some of her queenly privileges; she begins to rule sweetly over the powers of soul and body. Here wisdom comes to her assistance, enables her by sympathy with the Godhead to judge rightly of the supernatural state, and attain perfection. Next, counsel, judging of things that are difficult in the moral order directs the soul to choose that which is wise and prudent. In a very special way fortitude is needed to strengthen us to fight against aridity and distractions, and that tediousness, which nature necessarily experiences in the way of persevering. Here too, fear of the Lord will assist us to do our best, lest we lose the glorious prize of the eternal crown, and forfeit our right to the Beatific Vision. In the trials attaching to prayer it will assist us to remember what St. Francis de Sales has very justly remarked: Even though we be but statues in the house of the Lord, and apparently have neither light nor love, scarcely even life, we fulfil a noble end, we give God the glory He expects of us. And lastly, piety will teach us to look on God as Our Father, and whether He consoles or scourges, He does it for our own good, and to ensure us a rich reward in the life to come.

This, as we can easily judge, is a high degree of prayer; in fact, there are very great Saints in heaven, so St. Francis de Sales tells us, who never enjoyed any other form of prayer.

ANOTHER ELEMENT

There is another element of this prayer which we must not pass over. It is that during this prayer there is an *infusion of divine light*. Perhaps it is best to quote here from Fr. Gabriel's

St. John of the Cross (p. 120) for no one has insisted on this more than he:

"We want to determine precisely what is the manner of this infusion. We know, especially from St. Teresa's description, that infused contemplation has often an experimental character; the soul is aware that God is acting in it. Here, on the contrary, the infusion shows a markedly different characteristic: *It remains hidden*. St. John also explicitly says that. He calls this prayer: a hidden beginning of contemplation, obscure and arid for the senses, hidden and secret even for him who is receiving it."[1] All this we readily admit, provided it be the result of the *ordinary* action of the gifts of the Holy Ghost; for were it *extraordinary* it would be *infused* not *acquired* contemplation.

A SUGGESTION

It will assist us to remember that while this form of prayer is within the reach of all, there are some minds so very active, some imaginations so volatile that they cannot easily be simplified, and brought to one particular act of the will, one particular act of love. Such souls should not force themselves to adopt a method that is not suitable for them now. Let the imagination have its images, let it dwell sweetly on the Passion of Our Lord, or an act of the Blessed Virgin, and when it has been satisfied, both the will and intellect will get an opportunity of pursuing their way. To crush the imagination completely would only cause it to rebel the more. Still, there cannot be very much difficulty in acquiring this form of prayer, for St. Francis de Sales says it was the form of prayer which those who joined the Visitation Nuns very soon acquired. It is the prayer those in contemplative Orders are taught to cultivate, for by means of it one can pray easily at all times.

[1] Quoted by permission of Mercier Press, Cork.

THE ADVANTAGES DERIVED FROM THE
PRAYER OF SIMPLICITY

What precisely are the advantages to be derived from such a method of prayer?

In the first place, it advances us considerably in the love of God, because by means of it we can easily keep ourselves habitually in the presence of God. When practised for some time it creates a *state* in which we do our actions to please God alone, seize each opportunity, as it presents itself, of practising virtue, and enables us to advance rapidly towards perfect conformity with the divine will. It is, for souls called to sanctity by the active life, the prayer of the unitive way. How many who when in college were well instructed in making meditation have afterwards abandoned the practice? And always to their own disadvantage. And why? Because they did not know how to advance to this easier and sweeter method, in which they would have found the ideal they cherished, and to which they would have been drawn with an ardent desire.

In the next place, if we practise this form of prayer we shall, on coming to pray, find ourselves recollected. Because of this, the priest will say Mass more fervently, the Religious read the Office better, and all will daily advance from virtue to virtue.

In the third place, when the individual making prayer has been fully instructed in regard to the duties of the spiritual life, has become habituated to their practice, and is in the dispositions to make use of what has been learned—and these are always supposed when there is question of adopting this form of prayer—then the mind takes in a crowd of facts at a glance, and this inflames the will with an ardent love for God, which leads to detachment from creatures, self-sacrifice, and the practice of all the virtues. This makes work easier and more meritorious. It colours our life, and gives it a supernatural outlook. If followed courageously it leads to heroism, and this is the ideal of sanctity.

Lastly, if we follow this system, we shall cultivate a sweet and peaceful spirit, that will give that calmness to our lives which is the privilege of the Saints.

A QUOTATION FROM ST. ALPHONSUS

"*Active Union*," says St. Alphonsus,[1] "is perfect uniformity which the divine will, in which certainly consists the entire perfection of divine love, 'Perfection,' says St. Teresa, 'does not consist in ecstasy; but the true union of the soul with God is union of the human with the will that is divine.' This union is necessary, but not that which is *passive*, and 'it may happen,' says the same Saint (Teresa), 'that those souls which have *active* union alone, may have much greater merit, because they undergo greater labour, and the Lord directs them in this way, because they are strong.' The consolations, therefore, which they had not in this life, they shall enjoy in the next."[2]

[1] Praxis Confessarii: p. 253.

[2] *Note*: In making this quotation from St. Alphonsus it is not my intention to enter here into any of the disputes on contemplation that exist between the Thomistic and the Teresian schools. St. Alphonsus is a Doctor of the Church, whose works have been approved by the Holy See, and as such deserves our veneration. These considerations apply also to the note I here add on *infused prayer*.

As some who read this book will very probably enjoy this degree of infused prayer, they will expect, in a work treating of the love of God, some direction as to how they can make use of their state to advance in divine love.

This is extraordinary contemplation: it is infused knowledge of God and of things divine accompanied by infused love. This knowledge is called intuitive, being impressed on the mind by God Himself, and not being derived from the images of things. St. Thomas (Opusc. lxv) says of it: "In the lower degrees of prayer the soul loves and is loved, seeks and is sought, calls and is called, but in this degree by a wonderful and unspeakable process, it rises and is raised, seizes and is seized, presses closely and is tightly bound, and with a knot of love ties itself to God, being with Him as the alone with the Alone."

It is an *experimental* knowledge of divine things, produced by God supernaturally in the soul. It is termed *experimental* because we feel, experience God's presence spiritually, and remain passive. It is infused light and love.

We shall refer here to the four degrees recognised by all writers: prayer of quiet, full union, ecstasy and the transforming union. The effects these should produce, if genuine, are recollection, wonder, love, permanent peace, tenderness of conscience, humility, obedience, strength, hunger, thirst after justice, and an ardent desire for heaven.

Prayer of quiet. Before this stage is reached the soul, as a rule, passes through a severe trial, known as the *"night of the senses,"* which is a ray of the divine light falling on the mind, revealing its faults, showing it the depths of its corruption, yet inflaming it with love. It withdraws all sensible consolation or feeling of grace. This darkness is intermittent, and periods of intense delight come to assure and encourage you. You will profit by this state if during it you remain calm, do not indulge in making many or vehement acts, but quietly, and from time to time, abandon yourself to God's will, and make acts of love.

In this state avoid quietism which was condemned by Innocent XI, 1687. Above all, if attacked by temptations, resist them calmly, and reject them. When this infused prayer is not given, return again to the prayer of simplicity or acquired contemplation.

Full union. This is a state in which both the mind and will are absorbed by God. In it there are no distractions; the mind prays without images. Our personal effort is very little, and the soul must take care to follow the attractions of the Holy Spirit. It will experience jubilation, and a kind of mystical sleep, wherein it forgets self, resting peacefully on God's Heart. But the best mark to recognise it as coming from God, is transformation of conduct, and more fervent practice of virtue.

Ecstasy is a loss of the senses, resulting from the luminous vision of God's presence, and the intense union of love with the Divinity. In every genuine ecstasy there are given lights and revelations from God. The important thing, for him who would love God, is to put into practice what is inculcated by God, and what he clearly remembers is to be done. This will reform his conduct, make him submissive to authority, obedient to his director, and cause him to pray God to deliver him from false ecstasies, and all that is unbecoming or displeasing to Him.

Transforming Union. This is the highest union we can reach; it is uniformity with God's will, pure love, perfect charity. It is permanent, transforms the higher faculties, uniting them to God, and causing the soul to participate as fully as possible in the divine life. There is generally a permanent intellectual vision of The Blessed Trinity or of some divine attribute. Take care now to cultivate the pure love of God and perfect conformity with God's will.

Those who have the gift of infused prayer should, under the direction of their spiritual adviser, read "The Interior Castle," by St. Teresa. St. Alphonsus, speaking of a priest called to direct such persons, says: "The Confessor should have a thorough knowledge of the way to direct those gifted with contemplation, and so free them from all illusions, otherwise he will inflict serious damage on such souls." His own teaching on the subject is found in the "Praxis Confessarii" (pp. 245-262. Pub. 1748). It was reprinted in "Homo Apostolicus," Vol. III. pp. 127-142, and Gaudé has incorporated it in the Saint's Moral Theology: Vol. IV. pp. 598-610. An excellent work on the subject is that by Paschal P. Parente, S.T.D., Ph.D., J.C.B. Herder & Co.

CHAPTER IX

Consolations

ALL who have read the account of St. Peter, as outlined in the Gospel, will admit there is something very attractive about the First Pope; for be he represented as strong or weak, impulsive or failing in duty, he is always human, always eager to know the reward in store for him. In this way he shows at all times a practical turn of mind. This was particularly so when a rich young man was invited by Christ to abandon his riches, embrace poverty, follow the divine Master, and lay up treasures in heaven. The young man failed. He was too devoted to worldly goods to make the sacrifice. But St. Peter, knowing that the Apostles, of whom he was the leader, had acted differently, approached Our Lord, and said: "We have left all things and have followed Thee, what reward shall we have?" (Matt. xix, 27). Peter, in asking this question, presumably intended the answer to include temporal as well as spiritual favours; for where the Messiah was concerned the temporal was never far from the mind of a Jew.

Jesus made it clear what reward they were to expect: "Amen I say to you that you who have followed Me in the regeneration, when the Son of Man shall sit on the seat of His majesty, you also shall sit on twelve seats, judging the twelve tribes of Israel.

"And every one that hath left home, or brother, or sister, or father, or mother, or wife or children, or lands for My Name's sake, shall receive a hundred-fold, and shall possess life everlasting."[1] As St. Jerome[2] has very wisely pointed out, it is not

[1] Matt. xix, 28, 29.
[2] Book 3 on Matt. c. 19.

so much that these things are abandoned, for many pagan philosophers have left so much, but rather that they are abandoned out of love for God, that entitles to the hundred-fold here, and life everlasting hereafter. This conclusion some eminent writers draw from the words of Our Lord: "for My Name's sake" (Matt. xix, 29), "for My sake and for the Gospel" (Mark x, 30), emphasizing the fact that such sacrifices, *made out of love for God*, receive the coveted rewards. Both here, therefore, and in the life to come, two great rewards, consisting chiefly of spiritual favours and consolations, are granted those, who allow nothing to usurp the love of God in their hearts, and who are prepared to sacrifice houses, lands or even their dearest relatives, rather than betray the divine will, as expressed in the Gospels.

While we live on this earth, much happiness is the lot of him who loves God. St. John Chrysostom does not hesitate to say that if we take two persons, one of whom loves God, and the other does not, we shall find that the lover of God is, even on this earth, the happier of the two. He who loves God enjoys the peace of a good conscience, and knows that he will be able to continue for all eternity what he has begun here on earth; but the other is a source of trial to all, to Heaven which he has rejected, to the world with which he carries on incessant disputes, to his relations with whom he is seldom at peace, to his family, whom he is prepared to sacrifice to satisfy his depraved inclinations. Such a person seldom has a day's happiness; he seems to drag after him the dark clouds of discontent, and has a foretaste of eternal woe.

The all-important reward unquestionably is that of eternal bliss: no other than God Himself, as is frequently promised in the New Testament to those who love God (Matt. xix, 16, 17; xxii, 37; I Cor. ii, 19; I Ep. of St. John iv, 9, 10). This is an infinite reward, granted to merits, i.e., to the love of God reigning in the heart at the moment of death.

Another thought calculated to fill with happiness one who sincerely loves God is that, by enduring the trifling sufferings of this life, he escapes eternal flames.

Moreover, such a soul may even escape the flames of Purgatory altogether, as it may be sufficiently purified to enter heaven immediately after death, or at all events, if any faults remain, they will be quickly atoned for in that place of purgation.

On another occasion, Our Lord appealed to eternal happiness as the chief reason why the seventy-two disciples, sent by Him to preach to the Jews, should rejoice: "Rejoice not in this that the spirits are subject to you, but rejoice in this that your names are written in heaven." (Luke x, 20). This is a subject well calculated to make hearts rejoice; for it means that for all eternity they escape the company of those who do not love. Satan, being commanded on one occasion to state who he was, replied: "I am he who does not love." In hell there is nought but hatred and suffering. What a privilege to have it in our power to make sure of our election and happiness by divine love!

PLEASURES AND DELIGHTS

God, when He resolves to draw a soul from the pleasures and vanities of the world, commences by bestowing on it the sweetness of sensible consolation. Some have professed to despise these spiritual attractions; but such is not the attitude of the Saints; they receive them with thanksgiving, and reject them only when there is danger of their coming between themselves and God. St. Alphonsus speaks clearly on this point: "Spiritual consolations are gifts which are much more precious than all the riches and honours of this world. And if the sensibility itself is aroused, this is to be dreaded only when it takes us away from God, but it is very well ordered when it unites us to Him."[1] St. Thomas teaches that such consolations are given us by God with the object of fortifying, and so assisting, us to persevere. Such also is the teaching of St. Teresa, and St. John of the Cross. The latter urges us to withstand it only when attachment to it would prevent us reaching the higher states. Otherwise, he asserts, it is good. In fact Innocent XI has, it would seem, condemned the opposite teaching; for he condemned a proposition of Molinos, which discouraged any seeking after consolatory devotions. No; the Church, while urging to pay the respect to God that is His due, does not wish us to adopt restraint in the presence of a loving Father. In many of her prayers, she asks for an increase of light, a facility in doing good, a taste for heavenly things, and frequently invokes the Holy Ghost, the Comforter, to inflame our hearts with the delightful fire of divine love. We read in many places of the Scriptures that we should ask for and appreciate such consolations; in fact they are God's way of manifesting that He is pleased, and that He wishes to strengthen us for greater combats: Ps. 93, 16-19; Acts of Apostles ix, 31; 2 Cor. i, 3, 5, 6, 7; Ep. to Philemon, 7.7; etc.

Indeed, human nature needs some attraction of this kind; for as the senses are naturally drawn to and absorbed in what appeals to them in the world, their material tendencies must be counteracted by what is spiritual. The eye gazes with rapture on beautiful objects, the ear delights to listen to sweet music, the tongue appreciates the taste of good food, the touch is pleased by contact with soft garments, and the sense of smell by the odour of precious ointments. Now, no one says that these of their nature are sinful; they are dangerous, may incite to lust, and may weaken our power of resisting evil. Only in this way may we state there is in them a subtle poison. But sensible consolations, coming directly from God, and being

[1] *Practice of Loving Jesus Christ*: c. xvii, n. 21, 22.

more powerful than worldly pleasures, attract the senses and then the mind with greater suavity to the things of God. To relinquish what is dangerous, and rejoice in the sensible consolations that come from God, is positively delightful. These come abundantly in the beginning of our conversion, but when they have united us closely to the Supreme Good, are gradually withdrawn; occasionally, however, they return to encourage us in the fight, and to persevere in the way we have entered. Yet we must seek for and use them in conformity with the divine will; for it has been frequently observed that those who become unduly attached to them, abandon all spiritual exercises when the honey of consolation is withdrawn. How little love of God would be in such a way of acting!

DIFFERENCE BETWEEN PLEASURES AND DELIGHTS

Sensible consolations commence in the senses, being placed there by God Himself. It requires such to conquer the allurements of the world, and inflame the heart with divine love. Whatever is not joyfully embraced cannot be of long duration. The starved faculties, realising that in God alone their true Good is found, learn to break with creatures, and seek refuge in the God of peace and joy. But self, as the following example will show, may also arouse pleasures. I have conceived an ardent desire to practise some mortification, and if I succeed in carrying out my resolution I naturally experience a feeling of self-satisfaction. This satisfaction indicates the source from which the pleasure has sprung. But the devil also, assuming the appearance of an angel of light, may awaken in the senses a feeling which very closely resembles the sensible consolation that comes from God. The soul is not long deceived. By their fruits you shall know them. Such works of Satan can lead to nothing but confusion and sin, for there is always in them a very insinuating and dangerous element, which, unless rejected, will terminate in sensuality, and most probably in sin.

Delights, however, are different from sensible pleasures, for they originate not in the senses, but in the mind. They are lights, coming from the spirit of Truth, that inflame us with divine love. If they be strong, they easily overflow into the senses, though generally this is not fraught with danger. Sometimes, however, there does arise a risk, which the Saints have not been slow to grasp, and against which they warn us. The lower appetites, eager to participate in the happiness reigning in the will by reason of the delights it enjoys, endeavours to drag those delights into the sensible appetite. This easily stirs up sensuality. Should this danger occur, and it is by no means uncommon with those who have given themselves entirely to God, it can be overcome by the two following means: (1) we must strive to restrict such delights to the intellect and will. But how? By making acts of love to God. These too will assist us marvellously in advancing in divine love. But (2) should we experience any ill effects which lead us to suspect that either our imaginations or evil spirits are endeavouring to commingle poison with the honey of spiritual joy, then we should humbly request the Almighty to be pleased to allow us to experience only such consolations as come directly from Him. The Blessed Virgin, who wishes us to profit by all the graces we receive, will, if we but pray to her, come immediately to our aid, and then we shall discover that such pleasures become more refined, or vanish altogether.

Let us not forget that such pleasures and delights are given us for a definite purpose: to strengthen us to advance in divine love. They often come to us on the eve of a great feast, when the fervour of the faithful preparing for Holy Communion is more intense than usual, or perhaps on the feast of some Saint to whom we have a tender devotion. As we advance in divine

love they become more frequent, until in the end they constitute
an habitual element of our state. When we use them well, they
advance us to a higher degree, and may even introduce us to
the state of heroic virtue, which is the atmosphere in which
the Saints continually move, where even the most difficult
works are done with delight.

We should, then, accept them with moderation, avoiding, on
the one hand, spiritual gluttony, and, on the other, disrespect
for God's gifts.

TWO EXAMPLES

Some, despite what has been said, will still find difficulty in
distinguishing between spiritual pleasures and spiritual delights,
and as I know from experience, it is better to clarify the matter,
since the latter more seldom lead to difficulty than the former,
I will give two examples, which will place the two in a light
which no one can mistake.

A young man had a vocation to the religious life, but when
he expressed a desire to become a member of the Congregation
on which he had set his heart, was so thwarted that he considered
it better to postpone his entrance till opposition had died down.
In the college to which he had gone, he had met with success in
his studies, and for some time had thought of undertaking a
position in the college where he was. Suddenly he met with a
great cross. It staggered, but did not cause him to lose his peace
of mind. In the evening on which it occurred, he was attending
an entertainment when a wave of sensible consolation swept
over him. In a moment he realised the vanity of all things
earthly, the happiness of serving God, and the obligation he was
under to follow his vocation. Before the concert was over, he
had finally made up his mind; he never changed nor did he ever
forget the grace God had so liberally bestowed. This was an
example of spiritual pleasure.

Now, for an example of spiritual delight. One day this same man, kneeling before the Blessed Sacrament, began to reflect on the wonderful mystery of the Incarnation. He beheld in his mind's eye the Divine Infant, lying helpless and despised, in a manger at Bethlehem. Then he realised Who this was: the Second Person of the Adorable Trinity. What an infinite act of love on the part of God, to assume human nature to redeem mankind. No created intellect could grasp it. The human mind could only admire and wonder in presence of such merciful kindness. From all eternity God, in His wisdom, had thus determined to rescue the human race from the slavery of Satan. This thought made a deep impression on him, and he began to burn with intense love of God, and this left him for three days under the influence of the consideration.

This was spiritual delight, a favour bestowed by the Holy Ghost through the gift of understanding. It threw a flood of light on the sublime mystery; it illumined the intellect; it inflamed the will.

TOUCHES

Those accustomed to read the writings of St. Alphonsus will have noticed how frequently he refers to spiritual *touches*, that come from God, and how strongly he recommends us to profit by them.

But what do we mean by this interior touch? It is an act of the mind, by which we realize from the grace given us by God, that He has united Himself to us. We have felt His Presence, and the result is the consolation, the delight we experience in the heart.

Such touches are free from the dangers that accompany visions, locutions, etc. The safer method to pursue in regard to the latter is to take no heed of them; for if they come from God they will attain their end more quickly and surely the less we meddle with them. Touches, on the other hand, we should gladly cultivate. They come like a flash, and leave behind a delightful impression. They bestow an ardent desire to acquire holiness; they induce us to practise conformity with God's will. They are in perfect harmony with a pure and vigorous faith; and though sanctity does not consist in the mere enjoyment of consolations, yet we know from experience that souls generally make little advances in the ways of divine love, unless they receive and profit by them.

Scaramelli has justly stated: "Just as one body touches, or is touched by another, and so perceives its presence with pleasure, so the same, touching or being touched by a spiritual substance, perceives its presence in the act of the pure spirit, and with very great pleasure, if the substance touching be God Himself."[1]

THE SOULS WE SAVE

There is a thought which at any time will suffice to flood our hearts with joy. It is the number of souls, he who gives himself unreservedly to divine love, will snatch from the claws of Satan. Oh! how the demons exert themselves to prevent him making efforts to acquire charity, knowing that if he succeeds in attaining the perfection of love for God, he will bring thousands to Paradise. It was said of the Curé of Ars that he was instrumental in rescuing 80,000 souls from perdition, and of St. Teresa that by her prayers and good works she brought 60,000 to eternal happiness. It is recorded of John Baptist Stoegar, a Redemptorist lay-brother, who never ceased to pray, that "this Brother saves more souls by his prayers than all our Fathers by their preaching." So will it be with all those sincerely devoted to the interests of Christ; they shall find to their delight what an extraordinary number of souls they have rescued from hell. In each of these

[1] Dir. Myst. Tr. 3, 26.

souls they will see their own love personified. How such souls will thank them throughout eternity! And how God Himself, Who is never outdone in generosity, will reward them above measure![1]

THE ANGELIC CHOIRS

Let us not forget we have the denizens of Paradise, bright spirits, all mind to know and heart to love, witnesses of our struggles, who at any moment we call on them, are prepared to come to our aid. Besides, some of them are appointed our Guardians, and eagerly rescue us from danger: "Their angels in heaven always see the face of my Father, who is in heaven." (Matt. xviii, 10). These blessed spirits, ever beholding the divine essence, learn what they are to do in our regard and execute it lovingly. We should strive to imitate them in the pure love they bear God. In them there is no mixture of selfishness. We should imitate them in the great victory they gained, when Satan, proving a coward, fell from divine favour. We should pray to them for the grace to love God with that affection for which they are remarkable.

What have these holy spirits most at heart? To promote the divine glory. And how do they achieve this? By inspiring those of whom they have charge, to act always from the motive of divine love and so make every act an act of the love of God.

[1] There are many other consolations, which to describe fully would only overload this chapter with details. I shall refer to a few: The sacraments, which advance us from one degree of love to another, till we reach its personification in the Eucharist; the sacrament of Penance, which purifies souls, and Confirmation that makes them strong and perfect Christians. Then we have the good example of the fervent around us, ever inspiring us to lead better lives. Next we have good books, and respectable places of entertainment, etc., all of which indirectly assist us in loving God. And lastly we have the continual round of the festivals that occur in the Catholic Church during the year, reminding us of the glorious country, heaven, where we shall be able to love God to our heart's content.

LOVE TRANSFORMS

"Love draws, love conquers, love reigns," and when it is supernatural it transforms us, making our wills one with God's will. Surely such a thought should fill us with intense delight; for what greater blessing could be ours than to be so closely united to the Infinite Good as to become one with Him. In Him we find our most cherished desires realised, and clinging to Him we are made, though poor and wretched, really rich and happy.

Yes, truly love transforms; for it makes us "put on the Lord Jesus Christ" (Rom. xiii, 14), and then, by God's grace, we shall say with the Apostle: "Nor height, nor depth, nor any other creature, shall be able to separate us from the love of God, which is in Christ Jesus our Lord." (Rom. viii, 39).

CHAPTER X

Desolation and its Remedy

PATIENCE

ST. JAMES, in his Epistle, sang the praises of patience, when he wrote: "Patience hath a perfect work, that you may be perfect and entire, failing in nothing." (Jas. i, 4). The Greeks, who seem to have the correct reading of this passage, explain the text as follows: "Let patience be with you always, even to the end of your lives, so that you may be perfect, failing in nothing," from which it is clear that patience, if practised continually, brings us to perfection. In this way it can be reconciled with the Latin reading, which means: "Patience attains perfection, making you excel in virtue and good works, and at the same time freeing you from your faults." If patience,[1] however, is to attain its end, we must give it full scope by constantly enduring the evils that befall us.

But how can we say that one virtue alone can achieve so glorious a result? Because, as St. Gregory says, it is the root and guardian of all virtues; from it they all spring, by it they are all protected, so that it becomes the means of acquiring perfection. Does it not demand a vividness and strength in faith to see in the trials of life favours that are to be regarded with fondness and respect? Does it not require much prudence to preserve one's peace of mind, when buffeted by the winds of misfortune, and overwhelmed by the waves of a stream against which we

[1] What bearing, it may be asked, has the practice of patience or of the other virtues, on charity? They have a very important bearing *indirectly*; for they are the props of charity, assisting her to become perfect. This applies particularly to advancement in virtue, which will be treated in the next chapter.

are struggling? Does it not call for modesty, meekness and humility, to accept cheerfully the cold and bitter expressions of another's ill-will? Unquestionably. We can therefore safely say that by patience the practice of all virtues is ensured.

WHAT IS PATIENCE?

Patience is the virtue by which we are enabled to bear with calmness and peace such sufferings of life as do not cause death. I have said *"which do not cause death,"* for fortitude is the virtue that strengthens us to remain unduly perturbed when enduring the pains that do cause death. But patience controls that natural sadness, arising from present and passing evils. This sadness, once it destroys peace and happiness can, when immoderate, work dread ravages on the mind and heart. When not mortified it increases pain, which so annoys and disturbs, as to lead us into a thousand faults. These faults cause abundant graces to be withdrawn, and as a consequence diminish our relish for spiritual things. But, on the other hand, when sadness is absent, there is a joy which dilates the heart, renders difficult works easy, spreads abroad a happy and tranquil spirit, and brightens the countenance, as it reflects the peace reigning within.

ADVANTAGES OF PATIENCE

The blessings flowing from patience are so numerous that we must be content with mentioning but a few.

Our Lord, speaking of the sower, who went out to sow seed, tells us all the seeds sown, with the exception of one class, perished, and they failed, not because they were infertile, but because of the ground on which they fell. Some of these seeds flourished for a while but were ultimately lost from want of moisture, others because they were eaten by the birds of the air, others again because they were choked by thorns. But that which fell on good ground flourished; for it sank into "a good and very good heart, which hearing the word, kept it and brought forth fruit *in patience*." (Luke viii, 5). It was patience then that caused the word of God to fructify and merit heaven.

In the next place, patience, by keeping the mind in peace, preserves it in a state of recollection, and enables it to seize each opportunity of practising virtue that presents itself, and such occasions are unceasing.

Again, by patience we practise charity towards our neighbour, and give that edification, which is more powerful to convert sinners, than many sermons. St. Ephrem, a Doctor of the Church, who flourished in Persia during the fourth century, tells us that St. Abraham, a recluse, was ordered by the Bishop of the place to abandon his solitude, go to a neighbouring town, and preach there to its inhabitants, who led very indecent lives. When the Saint heard of the command his humility received such a shock that he requested the Bishop to excuse him from carrying out the duty entrusted to him. But the Bishop insisted on the Saint doing as he was told, so that Abraham at length addressed himself to the task. This, however, was a more difficult undertaking than he had suspected, for the people laughed him to scorn, turned a deaf ear to his exhortations, and at length seized and bound him, dragging him through their town till he was half-dead. Then they cast him away. The holy man, however, bore the ill-treatment with marvellous patience, never uttering a word of complaint. Finding himself neglected as he was, he betook himself to prayer, and prayed long and fervently for the conversion of his persecutors. At this he continued for some years, and then the people, incited by curiosity, came trying to discover what exactly he was doing. When they beheld his spirit of prayer, his perseverance, his unfailing courage, they were moved to pity; and being struck with remorse, responded to grace, and were reconciled with God. The Saint, seeing his mission had now turned out a success and that he had completed the task given him to do, arose early one morning, crept silently from the place, and returned to his beloved solitude, where he continued his life of prayer and mortification. It was his patience that had gained the victory.

Moreover, we must not forget the great rewards, granted both in this life and in the next, to those who practise patience fervently. The soul that in its patience follows the example of Christ, Who in His poverty, sufferings and death, was most patient, will certainly be richly blessed by God. This virtue will enable it to tread in the footsteps of the saints, who, like the Apostles, rejoiced under persecution, because "they were accounted worthy to suffer reproach for the name of Jesus." (Acts v, 41).

In the last place, even people of the world realise that if, as lawyers, doctors, or business men, they are to succeed in temporal affairs, they must practise patience. Now, if men and women in their daily affairs suffer so much in repressing their feelings to gain a passing applause, or the wages that are their due, what should we, the followers of Christ, be prepared to do to gain eternal glory, and win immortal souls?

THE PRACTICE OF PATIENCE

In practising patience, we must, in the first place, strive to endure the trials of life. These come directly from the hand of God, and are considered by divine wisdom to be the best remedy to heal our diseases. They are poverty, suffering, a severe cross that falls to our lot, the loss of a dear friend, the destruction of property, the failure of a law-suit, or, worst of all, the disgrace which one to whom we are closely related brings upon us. And strange as it may appear, it is really much better that such crosses fall to our lot, than that they do not. Perhaps we have been drifting into tepidity, are growing even cold in our spiritual life, are inclined to make for ourselves here a lasting city, and it is only some such trials that recall us to duty, expel pride, ambition, self-deception, any of which might lead to eternal ruin.

But perhaps what annoys us most is that this cross comes from our fellow-men, whose lives are far from edifying, and who even now are rejoicing at our discomfiture. Well, let us not forget that those who inflict this are but instruments in God's hands. True, we may not have deserved it; it was unjust that another got the verdict in his favour, because he was wealthy. Very well, but still Our Lord suffered greater injustice than we, and offered it for the salvation of mankind; and besides, if we do not deserve it now, perhaps in the past we so acted as to deserve a much severer chastisement. Now, it is precisely this injustice, so hard to flesh and blood, which is the marrow of the holocaust, and brings us the greatest merit. Had we been guilty, we should have deserved it, and could expect a poor reward, but being innocent we shall receive an ample recompense.

But we may still add: What has been said is true and at times I realise it quite clearly, but at other times I feel in a rebellious mood, grow disheartened, and understand I am not acting well. Yet perhaps even in this case we have done much better than we imagine; for though we felt the severity of the situation, we have not given way to self-praise. We have had our moods, indeed, but that is quite natural, for nature does not move on straight lines. At one time we are enthusiastic, at another down-hearted, at one time recollected, at another distracted, at one time fervent, at another cold, now rejoicing because of what has happened and again, because the same thing has occurred, we are peevish and sulky. Still the feelings here are not the guide to reveal what is right and what is wrong: that guide is faith, the teaching of the Church, conscience: "Our glory," says St. Paul, "is the testimony of our conscience." (II Cor. i, 12).

OUR FAULTS

After making some headway in the spiritual life, having mortified the senses and passions, having clipped the wings of our
imagination, and succeeded somewhat in restraining our minds
from wandering at prayer, we are disappointed at seeing ourselves fail from time to time in the practice of virtue. But the
remark of St. Francis de Sales will encourage us: Did we know
our weakness as well as the Lord does, we should not be disheartened at a slight outburst of temper, a retort, a peevish
complaint, an act of impatience, rather we should thank God
for His grace in preserving us from greater falls. Let us bear
well in mind that the offspring of Adam, conceived and born
children of wrath, cannot, since they have not the special
privilege granted to Our Blessed Lady, avoid all sin. We can
of course avoid all mortal sin, can, as we have already stated,
avoid all deliberate venial sins, and, if we are vigilant, lessen our
partly deliberate faults.

To labour at conquering these is an act of pure love. In the
beginning we make little headway, so that the Imitation says:
"Let us lay the axe to the root, that being purged of passions,
we may possess our minds in peace. If every year we rooted
out one fault, we should soon be perfect men."[1] Surely there is
no one, be he wanting ever so much in fervour, but can do so
much.

God, in His wisdom, has left us our weakness. If we had it
not how proud and insupportable we should be, seeing that with
it we are very vain and self-asertive. Against it we must continually struggle. This combat keeps us on the alert, awakens
our fervour, and urges us to strive after a high degree of virtue.
Often did the Saints fall into faults of surprise, but these only
urged them to aim the higher. Besides, our faults make us more
considerate in bearing with others; why should we demand

[1] Book i, C. 11.

more of others than we do of ourselves? And yet if we are to judge by our criticism of those who have but slightly offended us, do we not, when in a sulky mood, practically demand heroic virtue of others, while we ourselves are quite satisfied to remain at a low level?

As it would be a mistake to be unduly disturbed at falling into these, it would also be an error of judgment to decide to neglect them altogether. We fall easily, but we also rise easily. There are some people so bubbling over with good humour that they never grow disheartened at a loss; they are irrepressible, and come up smiling as brightly as ever. Let us, in conquering our faults, imitate their excellent spirits.

ARIDITY

In the last chapter we spoke of consolations, and gave the reader to understand that they do not always accompany prayer, nor the practice of virtue. They certainly suffer eclipses, and sometimes disappear for a long time, returning only at intervals. Aridity takes their place. Very likely we look on this as an evil, a positive drawback to our spiritual life. But strange as it may seem, this dryness, making its appearance at prayer, in our thanksgiving after Holy Communion, and in our visit to the Blessed Sacrament, so far from being a hindrance, is an advantage to him who is eager to love God. It may incline one to avoid prayer, but it is overcome not by following, but by contradicting our inclinations. The best remedy for it, as St. Ignatius tells us, is to prolong our prayer, and if we do it out of love for God, we shall find not only that it becomes easier, but advances us marvellously in divine love. When we act in this way we enter into the state of pure love, a state of the soul most pleasing to God.

But you may say: How am I to pray in this state? In the first place in coming to pray, resolve not to desire consolations, but to find out and obtain the grace to do the will of God. It would be well to make this a definite intention, as it will strengthen you to aim at the object you have in view. You may find it more convenient during prayer to make only short ejaculations, such as the following: "My Jesus mercy, Mary help," "Thy will be done on earth as it is in heaven," "Blessed and praised be God always," "I am delighted, O my God, that Thou are infinitely happy," "Blessed be the holy and undivided Trinity now and for evermore."

But to clarify this question of aridity, let me remember it may arise from a threefold cause. It may come directly from God, being sent to wean us from sensible pleasures, and advance us to a higher degree of divine love. In this case it should be considered a precious gift, and should be appreciated as such. With the fervent this will be always so. Without the slightest warning consolations will be withdrawn and aridity set in. It may, in the second place, be the result of some fault, to which we have grown accustomed, and because of which many graces have been withdrawn. This can be easily remedied by examining our consciences, and after discovering the offence to repent of it, and resolve to avoid it in future. In the third place, the devil, to disgust us with prayer and so lead us to its neglect, stirs up aridity. This last cause will be removed by prayer to Our Blessed Lady, St. Michael, or our Angel Guardian.

The reader may rest assured that to go from sensible devotion to aridity is a decided advance in the way of prayer. This is not by any means always clearly understood. Most people imagine that when they suffer aridity, they are cast off by God, forgetting that charity in its perfection is sanctity, and that love of God is shown, not by what we enjoy, but by what we suffer out of love for Him. It is to put off the things of the child, and put on those of the man; it is to partake of a solid and substantial food, which may not gratify the palate perhaps, but will be very beneficial to the growing man.

"Be renewed," says St. Paul, "in the spirit of your mind, and put on the new man, who, according to God is created in justice and holiness of truth." (Eph. iv, 23, 24).

To aim at solid virtue and to act generously with a humility free from discouragement, to continue to pray in spite of the repugnance we feel, to reflect with simplicity on the mysteries of Our Lord's life and Passion, to hope for great things, when we are weighed down by the weight of our miseries, and when divine justice seems to be crushing us, to abandon ourselves unreservedly into the hands of God, to follow Him to Mount Calvary, assisting Him to carry His cross—these are the foundation-stones on which the Saints have built the edifice of their sanctity. A soul who has never soared above this degree may be very holy and perfect indeed; for it is not beautiful thoughts make us holy, but the practice of solid virtue.

AN EXAMPLE

The Ven. Fr. Cafaro, one of the first companions of St. Alphonsus, a sketch of whose life had been written by the Saint, was certainly a man of extraordinary virtue, and far advanced in sanctity. Yet for six years previous to his death he was severely tried by spiritual aridity. To such an extent did this proceed that during meditation he could only repeat an ejaculation. Yet this did not cause him to grow discontented, nor lead him to abandon his usual devotions. Far from it; in these he was more exact than ever. He stated that saints are made by crosses, and certainly he made good use of the cross of aridity and desolation to advance rapidly towards perfection. Often did he experience such interior desolation that it seemed to him God had abandoned him. Yet he rejoiced in the superior part of his soul, for he was convinced that the love of God does not consist in sweetness, but in the accomplishment of the divine will amid bitterness. "The chief benefit of meditation," he would say, "is that it gives us strength to suffer, and so to please God. Patience then is the way to heaven, and we obtain it by meditation."

DESOLATION

Those who are anxious to love God must be prepared to remain with Christ on Calvary as well as on Thabor. After day comes night, and generally the brighter the day that has preceeded, the darker the night that follows: grief follows joy, winter summer, desolation delight.

Yet we should not fear desolation. If God is pleased to send it, it will be such as not to try us beyond what we can endure. It will be the sure means of conquering self, and of making love triumph.

There are two kinds of desolation: the little and the great. There are few in the world but suffer partial desolation at times; for it arises from the very nature of man. For instance, should we be tempted and delay in resisting the temptation we suddenly arouse ourselves, realise what we have done, and make an act of contrition. Then comes the harrowing thought; "Did I commit a mortal sin? I intend to go to Holy Communion to-morrow, and if I know for certain that I have now committed a serious sin, I am obliged to go to Confession before receiving the Holy Eucharist. O, my God! What am I to do?" Of course, if we can get a Confessor, he immediately sets our minds at ease, or if we have sufficient confidence to act on the principles already laid down for those in doubt, we shall see that since we ordinarily resist such temptations, we are free, when in doubt, to go to Holy Communion. But we shall suffer much anguish before laying the spectre to rest.

Such a trial as that described is but a trifle compared with the great desolation. This comes but seldom; in fact some never experience it, and even the most fervent and advanced pass through it only once or twice in their lives. Still it is well to consider it here, as it may annoy elect souls, and retard their advancement in divine love, though it is sent by God to attain an end directly opposed to the evil mentioned. It might even happen that such souls, growing disheartened, may turn away from the service of their Creator, and they who "have been brought up in scarlet," turn to feed on the offal of swine.

During this trial the soul may sweetly complain to God, saying: "I weep and my eyes run down with water, because the comforter, the relief of my soul is far from me." (Lam. i, 16). Several of the Psalms give beautiful expression to this state of the soul, and could at this time be read with much profit and consolation, e.g., (Psalm 68, 1-22): "Save me, O God for the waters have come in even into my soul, I stick fast in the mire of the deep, and there is no sure standing. I am come into the depths of the sea, and a tempest hath overwhelmed me, etc." The opposition from men is well described in verse 13: "They that sat in the gate spoke against me, and they that drank wine made me their song." Also, the Psalm Our Lord recited when He was nailed to the cross will be very suitable: "O God, My God, look upon Me: Why hast Thou forsaken Me?" (xx, 1-32).

This desolation is nothing else than the direct dealing of God with the soul. He will destroy in it the corruption of self-love, and lay an excellent foundation for attaining the heights of holiness, the prayer of union. As no one but God knows the corruption of our hearts, and the heights of holiness to which He calls us, so no one but Him can supply the remedy needed to achieve so desirable an end. In this state there are many temptations. St. Alphonsus, who passed through it triumphantly, was tempted against every virtue, and was rendered perfect in the practice of every one of them. There is a description of this desolation left us by the Saint:[1]

"God, desiring to purify the soul, to strip it of what satisfies the senses, and to join it to Himself with a pure love, has recourse to desolation, which, like a fire, burns into the soul, causing it to undergo, both interiorly and exteriorly, a very severe purification. He takes from it the knowledge of its condition, so that it does not even know if it is in the state of grace. It is surrounded by bitter darkness, and considers it cannot any longer find God. Nay, sometimes the Lord permits it to be attracted by serious temptations of the senses, or even by depraved notions of concupiscence, or thoughts of unbelief, despair, or hatred of God. It seems to be repulsed by God, Who refuses to hear its prayers. Then the devil on his part attacks it fiercely, stirring up temptations against chastity so that the soul is plunged in a night of darkness. Though the will rejects these allurements, yet the mind cannot decide whether it rejected or consented to them, and so it is in dread lest it has lost God, and it fears it is abandoned by Him, because of its infidelity."

Now, the timid will naturally say: "Oh! if the love of God costs so much, and demands such self-sacrifice, I fear I shall not be able to cultivate it."

But do not forget that even though you cultivate a fervent love of God, you very probably will never be called to endure such desolation; because it is given only to few, and to those who are well able to endure it. Besides it is accompanied by such a flood of grace, and the will is so strongly upheld by God, that Fr. Baker in his book, "Holy Wisdom," says there is little danger of consenting to sin. Moreover the trial is not continuous.

In truth this trial is a great grace from God, and the sincere lover of God will consider it such. We can, as St. Alphonsus asserts, console ourselves with the thought that God grants

[1] Practice of Loving Jesus Christ, C. XVII, 21, 22.

such favours only to His dearest friends, Whom He intends to advance to a high degree of holiness. If we pass through it courageously, and fervent lovers of Jesus and Mary always do, we shall be delighted that God gave us the opportunity of testifying our affection for Him, and shall always consider this night of darkness one of the most glorious stages of our earthly career.

CONSIDERATIONS TO ENCOURAGE US

The difficulty we have in the great desolation is to convince ourselves that all is well, that things were never better than they are now. We fear we are lost, and we fear that things will never come right with us again. This is the very marrow of the sacrifice; this is what burns out the dregs of self-love, self-esteem, and self-will. Without this searing, the sore would never be burned away nor healed. But let us consider the following, and we shall see there is no cause for alarm.

(1) It is absurd for anyone to say he knows he is lost; for all people can, by divine grace which is given abundantly to those who ask it, repent of sin, enter on a holy life, and become Saints. Some of the greatest Saints have, at one time, been the greatest sinners, e.g., St. Augustine, St. Margaret of Cortona, St. Camillus, etc. The Lord Himself, by the Prophet Ezechiel (xxxiii, 11), says: "As I live saith the Lord God, I desire not the death of the wicked, but that the wicked turn from his way and live."

(2) God rewards and punishes souls according to their works: "The Son of Man will render to everyone according to his works." (Matt. xvi, 27). If I am resolved to practise virtue, and correspond faithfully with grace, I shall not only save my soul, but merit a high place in heaven: "Confirm O God, what Thou hast wrought in us." (Ps. lxvii, 29).

(3) If after examining my conscience I cannot say for certain

I am in the state of serious sin, I can safely reject the matter as a scruple. Besides, were my soul covered with a hideous leprosy of sin, I can, by an act of contrition, remove the stains immediately, and become a friend of God: "Create a clean heart in me, O God." (Ps. i, 12).

(4) Many of the Saints have passed through trials much more severe than I have to endure. If I read the life of St. Catherine of Siena, or the life of St. Alphonsus, I shall be convinced of this; they came forth victorious; so can I.

(5) When my director assures me nothing is wrong, I must strive, in a spirit of faith, to receive his word as the will of God. In this way I shall preserve peace. "An obedient man shall speak of victory." (Prov. xxi, 28).

In all this period of desolation the director will do his utmost to console the one who undergoes it, and will keep as confidential what is submitted to his decision. It is a secret committed to his judgment, and if it be kept from others, the one who is enduring it will find it much easier to win through.

What is most important, however, about desolation is not exactly that we have endured it, but that we have suffered it well, and profited by it. If we have been patient, humble, obedient, and resigned to God's will, we may be certain that the trial will be much to our advantage; if on the other hand we complain, refuse to obey, are self-willed, we shall gain little by the great favour the Lord has bestowed.

NERVOUSNESS IS NOT DESOLATION

Some who suffer from a vivid imagination may consider that nervousness is the desolation here described. No; the two are quite different, and can be distinguished by the effects desolation produces, and the symptoms that accompany nervousness. We have described desolation, and need add nothing more. As regards nervousness it arises very often from ill-health, worry, anxiety, and over-work. It is a kind of a disease; for a weakening of the system has set in. *Still it is not a serious evil,* and should not be aggravated by the vagaries of the imagination. If the one who suffers from nervousness puts trust in the mercy of God, eats his food, aims at becoming strong, avoids self-pity, and struggles against the false notions that occur to him about his state of health, he will soon experience a marked change for the better. We must not forget that nervousness, when borne with patience, will advance us in the love of God; but on the other hand, if not well borne, will seriously retard us in this virtue.

It only remains to state, before concluding this chapter, that by describing the desolations as I have done, I am not confusing the two ways to sanctity. For not all who pass through such darkness, not even half of them, are called to infused contemplation; and St. John of the Cross[1] states he does not know why this is so. May we not suggest, with St. Teresa, that He keeps them for the more difficult way, that of a high degree of virtue, because they are strong souls, and will have more influence on the majority, who scale the ladder of perfection by advancing daily in virtue?

[1] Dark Night: C. ix, N. 13.

CHAPTER XI

Advancement in Virtue

It has often been asserted by authorities well qualified to speak on the subject, that some, who have conquered in desolation, have, by reason of some insignificant sacrifice they afterwards refused to make, withdrawn themselves gradually from the love and service of God, and have ultimately become castaways. We can all find in our own experience a parallel to this among lovers in the world. They have made many sacrifices to gain the affection of each other, they have looked forward to the day of their marriage, and yet a crisis, a trifle arises. One refuses to make a little sacrifice which the other demands. What is the result? The person who has been refused, is offended; a wound is caused, which daily grows deeper till in the end they drift apart, and do so for ever.

Now, it is to guard against such a disaster taking place, when God demands a little sacrifice, that we invite the reader in this chapter to consider the necessity of advancing in virtue.

WHAT IS VIRTUE?

But, in the first place, we must understand clearly what virtue is. Put briefly, it is a good way of acting.

What has been said of virtue is a good working notion of what it is; but it could be developed. This St. Augustine has done, and has given a very clear and beautiful explanation of it. He says: "Virtue is a good habit[1] in the soul, enabling him who

[1] St. Augustine: On Free Will. Book 2, He says, "Quality" of the soul, meaning of course "a habit."

has it to live uprightly and avoid evil." Such a virtue may be either natural or supernatural. When a habit is in harmony with reason, it is formed by repeated acts, and merits but a temporal reward, it is a *natural* virtue, but if the habit be infused into the soul by God, and gives the *power* to do acts that merit the Beatific Vision, it is *supernatural*. This latter must be guided by a supernatural motive, i.e., by a truth revealed by God. It gives strength and courage to the soul, making the possessor of it *manly* in the best sense of the term.

But if we are to cultivate virtue, we must dwell on some of the motives that urge us to practise it. In the first place, virtue brings peace, happiness and joy: for as St. Francis de Sales[1] says: "Nothing but virtue and devotion can make a soul content in this world." By practising virtue I gain the end God has designed for me; I render myself like Jesus Christ; I do what is pleasing in His sight. Our Lord, after giving a sublime example of charity and humility by washing His disciples' feet at the Last Supper, exclaimed: "If you know these things, you shall be blessed (i.e. happy) if you do them." (John xiii, 17). This happiness, found in the calm and secure possession of God's blessings, is obtained by practising conformity with God's will; this joy springs from the delight experienced in the soul of him who loves God. Yet the excellence of this conformity depends on the perfection with which we practise virtue. For, as already stated, the more patient we are in bearing suffering, the more humble in enduring humiliation, the more courageous in rejecting temptation, the more generous in assisting the destitute, the more self-sacrificing in promoting the divine glory, the more perfect precisely shall we be in our conformity with God's will. Nay, when we endeavour to practise virtue perfectly, accommodating ourselves to the circumstances in which we are placed, for this prudence demands, we have a

[1] Introd. to the Devout Life: Part V, C. II.

reflex of God's will in ours, we have uniformity with the divine will.

The thought of heaven is a very strong motive urging us to practise virtue. St. Alphonsus and St. Teresa declared in the clearest and strongest terms that their reward hereafter would depend on the way they practised virtue in this land of exile.

Omnipotent God, grant me the necessary graces to advance daily in the practice of virtue, even to the dawn of eternity, for then my heart will be one with the Sacred Heart and will be transformed into Christ, giving all for All, and reaping a rich reward in heaven.

PROGRESS IN VIRTUE

It is a first principle in the spiritual life that, if we fail to advance, we necessarily go back. We are like swimmers in mid-stream, with the torrent seething around us, and threatening to drag us to destruction. If we are not to be drawn with the current, we must fight strenuously. To fail to do so is to go back.

Let us consider how we are to advance in virtue.

God being infinite, has in Himself the perfection of all things. He has therefore in Himself the ideals of all the virtues. He is the model after which all that is good must be fashioned. These virtues are brilliantly reflected in the saints, and in holy souls. "We are his workmanship, created in Christ Jesus, in good works, which God hath prepared that we should walk in them." (Eph. vi, 10).

Exemplary virtues, of which St. Bernard and St. Thomas speak, are in the soul from the time it begins to copy the divine Model, Christ. Jesus Of course all virtues are infused with sanctifying grace, but they must be exercised and cultivated by imitating Our Lord.

These virtues, in their early stages, are chiefly concerned with the conquest of the passions. The inclinations of passion cease to be tyrannical only when the love of God increases and becomes perfect in the soul, and even then they will occasionally rebel. It is well to remember, too, that if the roughness of our character be removed, the infused virtues will act with greater facility; for such roughness is only too frequently a shelter for unmortified passions. If we are to succeed we must not forget to pray for the extraordinary graces needed to conquer them.

We know from experience it is more difficult to be exemplary in social than in private life. For somehow when we are in the presence of others, vanity, self-conceit, human respect exert themselves, destroying, if they can, the good intention, and urging us to indulge in the self-satisfaction which pride engenders. Because of this we are inclined to forget virtue altogether, or to adopt that which is merely natural. Then there are difficulties arising from business, from the pleasures and sufferings experienced in associating with others. These are not felt to the same extent by the solitary. Next, the ideals of the world are not the ideals of Christ. Worldly people have a cunning and dangerous method of ridiculing virtue. With persons of character this will serve to strengthen their courage, urging them to continue more valiantly on the way they have begun; but with the weak it will easily have the opposite effect, and turn them aside from virtue altogether. Then there are rivalries, jealousies, injustice, hatred, detraction, calumny and revenge, all of which are reflected in the conversation of the worldly, and create a pestilential atmosphere. It is certainly a great advance when, amid such surroundings, one does not change his course, but presses forward to the goal with the same zeal as when he lived in solitude.

Still we must, if we are to retain the respect due our state in life, and effect the good expected of us, adopt in public an attitude of propriety, which will be pleasing without being obsequious, genial without being familiar, and winning confidence without sacrificing principle. This may not be easy at all times, but experience will create habits in us, which we shall know we can follow if not with brilliancy, at least with tolerable success.

When we examine our actions, we shall discover that our weakness in virtue arises not from the virtue itself, but from the resistance of the will, from our want of firmness in determining to avoid evil and do good, from a desire to compromise with God. We have been obedient in some ways, but not in others; we have refused to pass certain limits because the interests of self-love dictated it. Now, I don't mean to insinuate that we found all this easy; we have indeed, but only at times, found delight in the abundant graces we have received and we had to bear with much aridity. However, if we are more generous in the future, we shall find His yoke sweet and His burden light.

PURIFYING VIRTUES

In the next place we have the purifying virtues. These, seeking God in all things, transcend the common ways of virtue and ensure a closer union with, and more perfect love of God. There is suffering here unquestionably; for such is the atmosphere in which the purifying virtues thrive. In this state earthly and dangerous affections and attachments are uprooted, not by force, unless it be the force which, like the gentle dew from heaven, acts softly on the soul.

This is the state in which great virtues are practised, and in which Saints are formed; for the trials of purgation give ample opportunity for perfect resignation to God's will. We have already dealt with desolations, which serve of course to purify the soul. But these piercing fires are kept alive also by temptation, persecution, opposition, failure, sickness, humiliation, degradation, and deprivation of friends, all of which God makes use of, to draw us closer to Himself. The bitterest trial of all is the persecution of friends, who are saddened at seeing the misery of our state, and at beholding the shattering of the hopes they entertained for our success, our advancement to honours, which would reflect on themselves. We, however, can afford to smile at such petty persecution, since in freeing us from all such snares, the Lord has bestowed on us the freedom of the children of God.

But God compensates us wonderfully, for now the soul begins to realise it can meditate, or better, perhaps, contemplate[1] with greater sweetness and joy. The half-hour we spend in conversing with Him, and to which we have looked forward ardently, seems now very short, and we could with much satisfaction prolong the time.

It is essential that during this period of purgation we do not be wanting in fidelity. This, however, does not mean that we do not commit faults. We shall have faults all our lives. But it means that we labour to conquer them, and refuse to make peace with them.

TWO OBJECTIONS

I can imagine someone say: What you state is very good, but how can we practise the virtues since we scarcely know even their names?

[1] It is the best to treat here a question we have so far avoided: the inadvisability of neglecting the practice of the virtues to follow an extraordinary way to which we are not called.

In practice we shall find, if we have much experience, that few are actually called to perfection by extraordinary ways. This is the teaching of the following masters of the spiritual life. St. Francis de Sales, Love of God, Book vii, C. 7: St. Alphonsus, Homo Apost. Appendix i, n. 16. St. Teresa, Way of Perfection, C. 17, and Interior Castle, 5th Mansions, C. 3, St. John of the Cross, Dark Night, C. ix N. 13; Alvarez de Paz. Works, Vol. III, p. 2, C. 4. Benedict XIV. Op. Omnia, t. viii, C. 26, 8; etc. This opinion is certainly probable, and very safe to follow.

We can reasonably conclude, then, that all should be fervent in practising virtue, and suspect whatever would tend to withdraw them from such a course.

To practise them one does not need to define and explain them. Many philosophers were able to do so, yet failed miserably in the practice of them. On the other hand, a poor old man or woman, who cannot define, may practise them perfectly. There are saints in every path of life; some of them are ignorant of letters, yet succeed in practising every virtue in an heroic degree. How? By the direction and assistance of the Holy Ghost. They know the virtues that pertain to their states—faith, hope and charity, justice, mortification, humility, chastity and persever-ance. Now should a temptation against one of these virtues arise, they advert to the danger of offending God, and resist the allurement, thus they practise the virtue; not, perhaps, very fervently in the beginning, but when the habit has been acquired, perfectly. Sometimes, however, the Holy Ghost, apart from temptation, will directly enlighten souls to practise virtues, and especially the virtue in which it is to specialise. The fervent gladly avail themselves of the opportunity of doing so.

The Holy Ghost is ever aiming at simplifying our spiritual life, labouring to bring all our virtues under one head, and this He succeeds in doing when He gets us to strive after perfect conformity with the divine will.

Another may, by way of objection, assert: "I have the gift of infused prayer; am I obliged to practise virtue?"

Of course you are, even though you had reached the stage of ecstasy, or even that of the transforming union. It would be fatal did contemplatives divorce infused prayer from the practice of virtue. It would be a sign that their so-called infused prayer was very far from being infused by God. St. Francis de Sales has positively stated that they who would act in such a fashion would be deserving of blame. Surely, out of gratitude to God for all the favours bestowed, such people should be very exact in imitating the example the Son of God gave them when on earth. They who fail to do so would fall from the heights to the depths.

All that has been stated in this chapter about advancing in virtue can be brought under the following heading: Be magnanimous, be large-hearted, be generous. This was the great virtue of the Saints; this they considered more important than ecstasy, the working of miracles or the announcing of prophecy. It urged them to do always what for them was most pleasing to God.

Christian magnanimity delights in doing what is difficult in the supernatural order. It rejoices in profound humility, in abstaining from food and drink, when these are not necessary, in cultivating extraordinary fervour at prayer, in exact observance of one's rule of life, and in ardent zeal for the salvation of souls. People devoted to this virtue remain unmoved amid the trials of life, compensate when they reasonably can, a favour bestowed with a greater than was received, and refer all to the glory of God. They are patient with the poor, affable towards the humble, indulgent with the ignorant, kind towards those wanting in confidence, and carry themselves with becoming dignity in presence of the great. They do not complain, are not obsequious, desire no revenge, and, in a noble spirit, despise being despised.

If there was ever a magnanimous soul, who imitated Christ closely, it was St. John of God. He made humility the foundation stone on which his virtue was built. Though poor, he never refused to assist those who asked for aid. His heart embraced all who were in suffering. St. Raphael, the Archangel, would come, in the appearance of a man, to assist him at his work. Our Lord, under the guise of a poor man, allowed Himself to be carried by the Saint to his hospital. He then made Himself known to St. John, and thanked him for all he had done, saying: "I consider as done to Myself whatever you do to My members."

THE PAGANS AND CHRIST

Pagan Philosophers placed the magnanimous man before themselves and their followers as the ideal to acquire. But their idea of the magnanimous man is quite different from that of the Christian. Our Lord, in His Sermon on the Mount, drew in bold and clear outlines, the true picture of the magnanimous man. He is one who labours, not for his own satisfaction, nor the praises of men, but for the glory of God; he practises virtue to gain an eternal not a temporary reward; he is generous, bears insults cheerfully, is not jealous, and if jealousy attacks him, crushes it as a temptation. If he sees another regarded as a saint he rejoices, since by this greater glory is given to God. In fine, he subjects the things of time to those of eternity.

But the magnanimous man of the pagans is by no means attractive, for he is proud, vain, self-centred, practises virtue only with an eye to his own advancement, thinking little of the glory of the God, or the welfare of his neighbour. He is simply the natural man, as perfect as the natural virtues can make him, but in many ways contemptible. He is unable, generally speaking, to withstand opposition, and very often follows his own inclinations. He would never dream of forgiving an enemy, and would consider himself a weakling did he not, when thwarted, burn with anger, and a desire for revenge. He knows nothing of humility, and could imagine no one capable of humbling himself before others but a slave. He is not an asset to humanity, scarcely a credit to virtue.

THE FEAR OF THE LORD

The ideal, sketched by Christ, is high: how can we live up to it?

We are assisted materially in "putting on Christ" by the gift of the fear of the Lord.

This gift we should take care to cultivate by corresponding with the inspirations that come through it from the Holy Spirit. Father Saint Jure[1] has said: "If we fail to exercise the gifts of the Holy Ghost we should praise and love God very imperfectly, do little or nothing heroic, and make but little progress towards perfection. The virtues sketch the picture, but the gifts give the finishing stroke. All the illustrious acts, and marvellous operations which raised the Saints to the heights of perfection, and of which we read in their lives, are the effects and production of the Holy Spirit."

This gift, the fear of the Lord, assists the virtue of hope in producing its acts with greater excellence. It controls the passions, uproots inveterate habits, strengthens us in the midst of adversity, and makes us courageous in the face of the enemy. It refuses to run unnecessary risks, will not expose a virtue to the danger of being destroyed or even wounded, despises the demons, and reverences with filial respect the Creator and Lord of all. Under the Old Law, it raised up men and women of heroic mettle, such as Isaias and Elias, Judith and the mother of the Machabees; and under the New Law it has produced such saints as St. Peter Damian, St. Bernard, St. Louis Bertrand, St. Catherine of Siena, St. Bridget of Sweden, St. Margaret Mary, and the innumerable band of penitent saints, all of whom are given us as models.

In this valley of tears we can never afford, even if the love of God reign unimpeded in our souls, to neglect the fear that arises from the judgments of God, the snares of Satan, and the treachery of weak human nature.

A STRONG MOTIVE

What more powerful motive could we have for practising a

[1] The Spiritual Life: p. 135.

high degree of virtue, and persevering in it till death, than the consideration that when the Church, with unerring accuracy, judges whether one of her children is to be raised upon the altars, she first decides: Did this person practise the virtues of Christ in an heroic degree? If the heroicity of the virtues is not proved, the cause is dropped; if it is proved, there are excellent grounds for believing the cause will ultimately be crowned with canonisation.

The Church then, with a divine instinct, considers sanctity consists in the practice of a very high degree of virtue, and this is acquired by frequently asking for the great graces needed, and then corresponding with them faithfully.

This means a sublime degree of the love of God, which not only enables us to practise virtue in a high degree, but which is rendered perfect by elevated virtues.

CHAPTER XII

Conformity with the Divine Will

There are very few Catholics, but have learned from reading good books, and hearing sermons, that our sanctification is to be found in fulfilling God's will.[1] Yet it would be more correct to say it is found rather in the way, the perfect way, we conform to the divine will. For some stricken with poverty, suffering or sickness, are obliged through necessity to submit to these trials, yet, because they endure them with a bad grace, never advance in holiness. It is only then, when we endeavour to carry out God's designs in our regard, that we give vitality to our conformity, and make it a means of reaping a rich reward.

THE DIVINE WILL

Faith obliges us to believe there is a will in God. "The Church," says the Vatican Council, "believes and confesses that God is infinite in *will* and in every perfection." The Scriptures speak frequently of God's will: "Who worketh all things according to the counsel of his will." (Eph. 1, 11). Our Lord in the Garden said: "Not My will but Thine be done." (Luke xxii, 42); and in the Lord's Prayer we say; "Thy will be done on earth, as it is in heaven." (Matt. vi, 10). But even though God had not spoken as clearly as He has, we could, as St. Thomas assures us, infer by reason that there is a will in God. We know God exists, and we can by reason alone prove He is an infinitely

[1] As it has been already shown that the sanctity of the soul is divine love, it follows that the means to attain sanctity is the means to acquire perfect love of God; in fact perfect conformity with God's will is perfect love.

perfect Being, an infinite spirit, with an infinite intellect, which understands its own perfections, and all things that exist, or could exist. In every nature that has an intellect there is a will; for a will is nothing else than a movement of the rational appetite to a good presented it by the mind. Since God has an infinite mind, He must have an infinite will. This will prohibits, counsels, prescribes and executes.

GOD LEAVES US FREE

We must clearly understand that God, in calling us to fulfil His will, does not act in a despotic manner, or as one would say, arbitrarily. The divine will is guided by the divine intellect, for as God by one act understands all things in His essence, so by one act He wills all things in His goodness. He has created each soul, knows its weakness and its capacity for achieving good. He has by His intelligence designed how each soul is to develop, and attain the perfection to which He has called it. All indeed must follow the divine Model, Christ Jesus, but all are not to do so in the same way. For as in nature there is an endless variety of flowers, each with its own specific form, odour and beauty, so among souls there is a wonderful variety. Scarcely shall we find two exactly alike. God desires each soul to reach its own perfection and glorify Him in the way He has designed, and Our Lord, by His death on the Cross, has purchased all the graces necessary to achieve this; now, the divine intellect embraces in our regard what God has designed. It commands, counsels, directs what is to be done. We can see then how wisely all persons act who labour zealously to gain uniformity or perfect conformity with the divine will. In all this God does not force us. But He draws us, for He has made promises unbounded in their generosity. Those He cannot violate, for He is divine Truth, and the truth of God is eternal. Let us call to mind some of these promises. We find them partly in the Old Testament, but chiefly in the New and in Tradition. These are some of them: God wishes all to be saved, and come to a knowledge of the truth. He gives sufficient grace to all, and abundant graces to those who ask for them. He has died to save all men; He will render, when He judges, to everyone according to his works; He is not a hard taskmaster, for He knows well the weakness of human nature, yet as heaven is an eternal prize, which can be won only by a struggle, He has made earth a place of trial. Merit alone is crowned in the life to come; we must strive lawfully, we must fight the good fight. This is the way to conform ourselves to God's will.

THE WILL OF GOD OUR SANCTIFICATION

It is a well-recognised principle in the spiritual life that conformity with God's will is sanctity. We can prove this by the following argument. God has designed the sanctity and merits by which we shall glorify Him in Paradise, and grants graces that we may attain them. This precisely is His will so far as our sanctification is concerned. Consequently if we obey His will perfectly, we shall reach the heights of sanctity.

We shall now consider what some, whose teaching is justly esteemed as worthy of the greatest respect, have said on this subject.

St. Alphonsus[1] says: "Conformity means to join our will to the will of God, but uniformity means to make the divine will and our will (morally) one, so that we will nothing but what God wills, and God's will alone is our will. This is the summit of perfection, to which we should always aspire; this should be the object of all our actions, of all our desires, meditations and prayers. For this we should beg the assistance of the Saints, our advocates, of our Guardian Angels, but above all of the Most Holy Mother of God, who was the most perfect of all the saints,

[1] Conformity with the will of God: p. 13.

simply because she, more perfectly than all other creatures, embraced the divine will."

Could language describe more clearly than the words of St. Alphonsus that the way to holiness is by conformity with God's will?

St. Francis de Sales[1] is equally emphatic in teaching the same doctrine.

"Whoever truly takes pleasure in God desires faithfully to please Him." He further adds:[2] "In finding out God's will we should implore the light of the Holy Ghost, apply our consideration to the seeking of His good-pleasure, take counsel with our director, and perhaps also with two or three spiritual persons, and then in the name of God make our resolution, and once resolved refuse to question our choice, rather keeping and pursuing it peacefully."

The next quotation we give is from St. Teresa,[3] who states:

"All that one who devotes himself to prayer has need to acquire is conformity of his own will to the divine, and he may rest assured that herein consists the highest perfection. Whoever practises this best will receive from God the greatest gifts, and will make most progress in the interior life."

Lastly St. Catherine of Siena, who was no dreamer, nor one anxious to compromise the truth, saw clearly that in fulfilling God's will, she could practise all virtues in a very high degree, and be ultimately transformed into God. One has only to read her short treatise on "The Divine Will" to see that she recognised it as the sure and easy way of reaching the heights of sanctity.

THE SIGNIFIED WILL OF GOD

Though there is but one will in God, we can say that, by

[1] Love of God: Book viii, C. 1.
[2] l. c. C. 14.
[3] Interior Castle: Man. 2. C. 1.

reason of the way it commands, there is the signified will, and the will of good-pleasure. It is called *signified*, because it has been made known to us, or signified by revelation. The will of God is also termed the will of *good-pleasure*, and embraces such visitations as sickness, ill-fortune and the other trials to which men on this earth are liable. The signified will we embrace freely, the will of good-pleasure we must endure. It is called the will of good-pleasure, because it has *pleased* God to visit us with something we cannot escape. Still into the will of good-pleasure the signified will enters, and renders it perfect. In the divine good-pleasure are the circumstances in which a high degree of virtue can be practised. St. Ludwina very probably would not have become the great Saint she did, had she not spent forty years on a bed of suffering. St. Stanislaus Kotska would not have reached perfection so quickly had he not, at the hands of a near relative, been subject to persecution and contempt. St. Margaret Mary became the Apostle of the Sacred Heart only after passing through a series of persecutions, which purified her, and rendered her fit to execute God's designs. St. Gerard Majella, by being wrongfully accused of an atrocious crime, advanced courageously to heroic sanctity.

St. Francis de Sales, speaking of the signified will[1] says: "God proposes to us clearly and in advance the truths He would have us believe, the goods for which He would have us hope, the pains He would have us endure, what He would have us love, the commandments He would have us observe, and the counsels He would have us follow. This is termed His signified will, because by it He indicates what He has ordained, and intends to be the objects of our faith, hope, fear, love and practice . . ."

The signified will of God, then, comprises a fourfold object: the commandments of God and of His Church, the evangelical

[1] Love of God: Book viii, C. 3.

counsels, divine inspirations, and for religious their rules and constitutions.

With regard to the counsels of the Gospel, it should be noted that we are not expected to observe them all; for some contradict others; it is God's will we observe those suited to our state in life. As the guiding star here is prudence, we should, to avoid falling into error, follow the advice of a learned, holy and prudent director.

Treating of divine inspirations, it should be stated, to avoid all scrupulosity, that, generally speaking, they do not bind under pain of sin, but if they are clear, make a deep impression, and leave no doubt in the mind, there would be some fault in neglecting them.

GOD'S WILL OF GOOD-PLEASURE

The divine will of good-pleasure is simply such things as proceed from God's will, and which we cannot escape. With regard to some of these we have already dealt at length, such as adversity, aridity and temptations. We shall dwell here on sickness, our natural defects and the pleasant occurrences of life.

In regard to sickness, on which we touched already, it must be admitted that of all the trials we have to endure this is the one in which, as a rule, we fail most. In this we are surprised, because on reading of the spiritual advantages derived from sickness, how it purifies the heart, enlightens the mind, humbles us beneath the Omnipotent hand of God, enables us to practise great virtues, and embellishes our crowns in Paradise, we may have desired and even prayed for sickness. But when, in the natural course of events it did come, were we not painfully aware of the fact that its poetry had vanished, its advantages had failed to make an appeal, and that we had been possibly indulging in day-dreams? In fact, did we not find it much more difficult o practise virtue in sickness than at any other time? Yet have we really failed after all? Did our ardent desires, the result un-questionably of grace, not produce some excellent results? Perhaps they did attain the end for which they were intended. For fervent desires are nearly always efficacious, and it would be impossible that, in the hour of trial some of their glow did not enlighten our minds, and warm our hearts. We may have expected that under suffering we would be in the same state as when, influenced by a strong grace, we were led to delight in suffering. But then we considered suffering in the abstract, here we are brought face to face with it in the concrete. To delight in the abstract contemplation of a trial, and to rejoice in the reality of it, are two things very far apart. The first is the beginning, the second the consummation of high virtue. Now unless we had already practised patience, had borne with-out complaint the trials of life, had rejoiced to bear suffering and contempt at the hands of our fellows, we could not, without a miracle, rejoice to bear sickness, and the many inconveniences that accompany it. We must bear in mind we have at all times to be patient with ourselves. In the beginning we must be content with poor results. At other times we shall, however, under a strong impulse of grace, make wonderful strides towards perfection, especially in bearing sickness. This success will more than counterbalance our failures.

Why, it may be asked, did God bestow the grace to desire suffering, if, when it did come, we could not bear it with joy? For several reasons, but especially for the two following: that we might be encouraged to bear patiently the trials of life, and so be strengthened to bear well those of sickness, when they come, and moreover that we might get a strong impulse to begin and pass through the intervening stages, and ultimately arrive at the point where we could rejoice in suffering.

It is certain that from sickness, as from any trial, we generally reap distinct advantages: we realise our weakness as never before, we are weaned from the delusion of imagining ourselves farther advanced on the way of sanctity than we really are, we see very clearly how absolutely we depend on God, and we grasp too how numerous and dangerous are the snares besetting our path.

NATURAL DEFECTS[1]

In the next place there are *natural defects*. Under this head are included want of talents, lowly birth, and want of ability in conducting affairs. Such defects are often allied with God's designs on our souls, and it is an act of faith to consider them as such. How many souls are now shining brightly in Paradise, because their footsteps were dogged by such defects! When such trials press heavily we should take care to conquer jealousy by humility, anger by meekness, chagrin by resignation to God's will. Such practice of virtue is perfect conformity with the divine will. At the same time we should take pains to conquer our defects. Great application can, as a rule, supply for want of talents. Many in the beginning of their studies are failures, but by close application become experts in what they have taken up. Lowly birth is scarcely a draw-back, since it makes us one of the democracy that is so lauded to-day. Want of ability in conducting affairs may be overcome by taking care to study what we have to do, realising where the danger is, and taking the means to avoid it.

On the other hand, how many by ability, wealth, beauty and success, have been drawn to perdition! Had they but cultivated the virtues necessary to counterbalance these gifts, they would have been more contented here, and more happy hereafter. To what advantage did St. Augustine, St. Bernard and St. Thomas

[1] How can natural defects, the reader may ask, have any bearing on our love of God? Quite simply; for they are a cross all our lives, and if we bear them well out of love for Him, they will certainly be an occasion of increasing divine charity.

employ their talents by subjecting them to virtue! What supernatural results did St. Louis of France and St. Aloysius Gonzaga
reap from their earthly possessions, the first by using, the
second by abandoning them! Consider how advantageously St.
Elizabeth of Hungary and St. Thérèse of Lisieux employed
their beauty, by preferring beauty of soul to that of the body.

PLEASANT HAPPENINGS OF LIFE

Lastly, we have occurrences which are pleasant, and in keeping
with our tastes.

Pleasant events[1] proceed from God's will, but when abused
cause untold ruin to the soul. Very likely more souls are lost
by abusing the favours God bestows than by neglecting to bear
trials with patience; for pleasures exercise on all men greater
influence than they are prepared to admit. The senses are steeped
in it, the passions aroused by it, even the will falls a victim to it,
so that success, talents, praise, the esteem of others, are often
seized on with avidity, because the pleasure is sweet, and
interests are advanced. We must, however, in all these matters,
abide by the golden mean. We must live in society, must assist,
console, and even humour one another, and we must be on our
guard not to imitate that rudeness, by no means virtuous, which
some devoted to virtue at times deliberately assume. Boorishness
is not virtue, and if not virtue it must be vice. Whatever means
we take of conquering our vain-glory, it must not be by rudeness.

No one is so foolish as to believe pleasant company, speeches,
and feasts are an evil; they are not; in fact, when properly regulated they promote a spirit of charity and forbearance. They make
the wheels of life run more freely. And indeed when praise is
offered, nothing more is usually meant than the congratulations
demanded by courtesy. When praised for what we have done

---

[1] Such events can be occasions of advancing in divine love; very often, however, from want of foresight and care, they cause the ruin of charity.

well, it is in good taste to say "I am glad you are pleased with it," and pass on to something else. Do not reject it in a rude manner. To do so will cause you the loss of a friend.

THE SACRED HEART AND THE WILL OF GOD

An easy and delightful way of acquiring conformity with God's will is union with the Sacred Heart of Jesus. To-day this is the most popular of all devotions; it appeals to all, satisfies the tastes and needs of all, and has brought incalculable blessings on the world. By uniting ourselves to the Sacred Heart, we unite ourselves to the divine will, for union with the Sacred Heart is union with God's will. This Heart is full of kindness, mercy and love, so that all sinners and saints, the just and unjust, the innocent and the penitent—can meet in this adorable Heart. If we make a mistake we can come to this Heart, and obtain forgiveness; if we are in aridity or desolation we shall find in It peace and happiness, and if we wish to advance to sanctity we shall find in It a never-failing fountain of grace and inspiration.

And united with It we shall find the Immaculate Heart of Mary, whose burning love, and fervent prayers, will aid us in making our hearts sweet images that will reflect the humility and meekness of Jesus.

GENERAL CONCLUSION

We have now traced the development of divine love in the soul from its inception to its consummation. We have seen there are two ways—the active and passive—by which it can be attained. The assistance of the gifts of the Holy Ghost is given abundantly to both ways, provided we are faithful in corresponding with divine inspirations. The Saints have always preferred the active way, as being that which is often more meritorious, and less liable to delusion from snares, set by the world, our own passions and the devil.

Yet both ways lead to the same conclusion—perfect conformity with God's will—uniformity—in which perfection consists.

The great consolation for everyone is that every soul is called to it. It is a life's work. If we begin prudently we shall the more easily persevere. Towards the end we make considerable progress in a short time, just as a heavy ball rolling down a hill increases in speed, till at the bottom it is brought to a stand-still.

May the God of infinite Majesty and Power grant everyone who reads this book efficacious grace to practise, both in life and in death, *perfect conformity with His will*, for this is the genuine love of God, in which true happiness is found.